WHY THE UNIVERSE IS THE WAY IT IS

HUGH ROSS

BakerBooks

a division of Baker Publishing Group
Grand Rapids, Michigan

© 2008 by Reasons To Believe

Published by Baker Books
a division of Baker Publishing Group
P.O. Box 6287, Grand Rapids, MI 49516-6287
www.bakerbooks.com

ISBN 978-0-8010-7196-6 (pbk.)

Printed in the United States of America

Library of Congress Cataloging-in-Publication Data
Ross, Hugh (Hugh Norman), 1945–
    Why the universe is the way it is / Hugh Ross.
        p.   cm.
    Includes bibliographical references and index.
    ISBN 978-0-8010-1304-1 (cloth)
    1. Cosmogony. 2. Creationism. 3. Biblical cosmology. 4. Creation. I. Title.
BS651.R767 2008
231.7′65—dc22   2008020162

12   13   14   15   16   9 8 7 6 5 4

Contents

Contents

Contents

Contents

List of Illustrations

List of Tables

Acknowledgments

This book was born from conversations with people whose names I may not know but whose faces and concerns I can easily remember. Perhaps *you* are among those who challenged me with a *why* question after hearing me speak at a university, workplace, church, conference, or some other setting. If so, thank you for thinking about God's purposes for the way the universe is designed and crafted and for stimulating my research. My colleague Fuz Rana was the first to suggest I put these thoughts into writing. He was also the first to review my earliest chapters and offer helpful suggestions.

I'm grateful for the skills of an outstanding editorial team, including my wife, Kathy. She spent three weeks in isolation, honing my original materials into a draft. Then, armed with feedback from our friend Rachelle Gardner, Reason To Believe's executive editor, Patti Townley-Covert, guided me through multiple drafts to enhance both the organization and the readability. Marj Harman, with the help of Linda Kloth and Maureen Bell, checked references and quotations and offered judicious feedback. Jonathan Price and Sandra Dimas gathered the figures and massaged the diagrams into finished form. In addition, Sandra, with help from our dedicated volunteer Colleen Wingenbach, did the copyediting and constructed the style sheet and index.

Several theologians and scientists reviewed the manuscript, and each contributed ideas for improving its content: Krista Bontrager, Dominic Halsmer, Craig Keener, Vern Poythress, Fuz Rana, Dave Rogstad, Kenneth Samples, Mike Strauss, and Jeff Zweerink.

My assistant Diana Carrée vastly expedited my research for this project by writing a program to organize all the materials cited in the book. She handled correspondence, sorted my stacks of papers, and aggressively protected my writing time. Her efforts along with my colleagues' willingness to absorb extra travel and speaking assignments kept this project on track.

My wife not only helped with the editing but also served as my main sounding board for the ideas expressed in this book. Kathy helped me transform complex principles and concepts into readable prose. I'm also grateful for her willingness to fill in for me in various ways, from household chores to social functions, so I could stay focused.

Every book I write takes a team to produce, and I thank God for the team he has given me. Our dear friends at Baker are also valuable members of that team. Special thanks to Bob Hosack, Kristin Kornoelje, and Wendy Wetzel for their contributions.

Introduction

Let's Play "I Spy"

This book is about purpose—actually *purposes*. Some are obvious, others veiled. Some remind me of the *Where's Waldo?* books my sons used to enjoy, or the "I Spy" computer games my young nephew plays. The purposes may be difficult to see, but they're there.

Many of the latest scientific discoveries bring these hidden purposes for the universe's existence, structure, and history into view for the first time. Seeing them helps explain why we're alive at this juncture in cosmic history. More importantly, it provides insights to humanity's ultimate destiny.

The most obvious purpose now recognized by the majority of astronomers for the origin, characteristics, and history of the universe is to provide a suitable home for physical life—humanity in particular. Famed British theoretical physicist Stephen Hawking described this observation in *A Brief History of Time*, the bestselling science book of all time:

> It would be very difficult to explain why the universe should have begun in just this way, except as the act of a God who intended to create beings like us.[1]

American physicist Freeman Dyson expresses this same impression:

> The more I examine the universe and study the details of its architecture, the more evidence I find that the universe in some sense must have known that we were coming.[2]

Hawking, Dyson, and many other distinguished physicists emphasize the realization that only in the context of human existence does the universe make any rational sense. *Why* this is so, however, puzzles even the greatest minds. Albert Einstein has been widely quoted as saying, "The most incomprehensible thing about the universe is that it is comprehensible."[3]

Some features of the universe, nevertheless, seem strangely contrary to what's "best" for humanity (see chapter 1). These incongruities cause many scientists and others to question whether or not the universe could have been divinely or benevolently designed to provide a home for life and humanity.

Over the past four hundred years of scientific research, a pattern has emerged that bears upon this question. It appears that even the best explanations for a phenomenon or system under investigation must acknowledge some anomalies, and yet these seeming discordances don't necessarily negate that explanation. The misfit findings simply remind us that human investigators lack perfect and complete understanding of any phenomenon or system we may study. Scientists also have learned that anomalies serve as springboards for gaining new heights of understanding. So far, most bothersome incongruities, once understood, reveal previously unrecognized purposes—benefits initially overlooked.

On a cosmic scale, researchers' experience with apparent inconsistencies implies that more purposes likely exist for the universe and its features than simply to provide life and humanity with a comfortable place to live. This book digs into these paradoxical features of the universe with the intent of uncovering their less-than-obvious purposes.

The goal of such excavation goes beyond satisfying my own and others' curiosity about the universe. I am firmly convinced that by discovering the intentionality behind the universe, we gain increasing insight into and confidence in the ultimate purposes for our own brief lives on this pale blue dot called Earth.

The first part of this book examines the widely perceived enigmas of the universe to determine from a scientific perspective each one's underlying significance for humanity's existence. These findings offer readers a fresh perspective, a new vista from which to contemplate why the universe manifests the puzzling features it does.

The second part of this book explores how the Bible accurately and uniquely described the major features of the origin, structure, and history of the universe thousands of years before any scientist discovered them. At the same time, the Scriptures stated both implicitly and explicitly the Creator's purposes for the universe and its attributes. The predictive success of biblical cosmology affirms the reliability of Scripture's message about why the universe exhibits the characteristics it does. The Bible is as relevant today as ever. Thus, Part 2 integrates the biblical explanation with the scientifically determined explanation of why the universe is the way it is.

This combination of scientific and biblical reasons for the universe and its features yields a solid foundation for the ultimate hope, purpose, and destiny of each and every human being. My intent in writing this book is to provide more than a measure of understanding of cosmic perplexities. I want readers to take away a renewed appreciation for the awesomeness of the universe and especially for the value—and eternal destiny—of their lives. Discovering the hidden purposes for the universe will stimulate an eager anticipation of all that lies ahead—beyond the universe we now see.

1

Why Ask Why Questions?

Self-preservation—it's a powerful drive we humans share with every other creature on the planet. In addition to being highly motivated to do whatever we can to preserve our physical lives and enhance our physical well-being, people express a motivation not seen in any other animal species—a yearning for a sense of purpose.

This urge compels humans to ask questions, BIG questions. In *A Brief History of Time*, Stephen Hawking, the world's most famous physicist, expresses this compelling desire:

> We want to make sense of what we see around us and to ask: What is the nature of the universe? What is our place in it and where did it and we come from? Why is it the way it is?[1]

Many people besides physicists yearn to know the answers to these questions.

The Search for Answers

The fact that you're reading this book says something about you. You're someone who hasn't relinquished the curiosity you were born with even though many people seem to let it go as they grow into adulthood. Why have you remained curious? Perhaps it's because you have some measure of confidence that meaningful answers can be found. Somehow that confidence—or longing—has been kept alive.

The fact that I'm writing this book tells you something about me. Curiosity is a driving force in my life—one so powerful it could have brought me to harm. While trying to investigate the structure of a hornet's nest, I learned the importance of a good throwing arm and fast legs. While venturing across Vancouver, Canada, on foot to explore the nearby mountains, I learned, sometimes the hard way, the importance of keeping track of the Sun's position in the sky and of setting up landmarks to guide my return.

Many people can recall similar experiences. These curiosity-inspired explorations suggest that human motivation to seek answers to their questions, big or small, may sometimes be even stronger than the powerful drive for self-preservation.

A simple *why* question launched my career in astronomy. One starry night when I was seven years old, I asked my dad and mom, "Are the stars hot?" (Though I don't remember the details, I suspect an earlier experiment involving a fingertip and a lightbulb prompted my query.) Their unified "yes" generated my second question: "Why?"

Wisely, my parents told me I could find the answers at the library. And I did. Books revealed some answers and prompted more questions. More answers led to still more questions. And that process continues to this day. Along the way I've discovered that *why* questions about the universe spring from two distinct sources.

Scientific curiosity arises from the desire to understand the way things work. People want to understand how things like gravity, electricity, and magnetism—as well as living organisms—function. That type of curiosity stimulated Newton's question about why apples fall to the ground, Darwin's question about why the finches on one of the Galapagos Islands had larger beaks than those on another, and my question about why the stars are hot.

Spiritual curiosity is driven by the quest for meaning and coherence. This source of cosmic *why* questions combines reason and imagination, logic and speculation. Some of these questions are simple (though not easy) and direct: Why do I exist? Why does anything exist? Why do I care? Even people whose daily struggle to survive leaves them little time, energy, and opportunity to pursue answers somehow can and do discover amazing insights that bring them a large measure of peace, contentment, and hope.

On the other hand, many people of great intellect, solid education, and substantial financial means neglect the grand questions of life. They complain about the state of the universe and their present predicament within the vastness of the cosmos without putting their resources to use in an attempt to find satisfying answers.

Though my family was poor by Western standards, we had a wealth of access to nature, to thinkers, and to books. And because my family never embraced any particular philosophy or religion, I had great freedom to explore the big questions of life. My neighborhood offered a rich diversity of Eastern and Western belief systems, spiritual and secular. As a teenager I read manifestos, philosophy texts, and many so-called "holy books" with the skeptical eye of a budding scientist.

After months of intensive investigation, I couldn't escape the stunning (and unique) consistency of the biblical texts with scientists' emerging discoveries about the universe, with natural history, and even with current events in human history.

Finally I had to acknowledge the obvious: no human mind or collection of minds alone could have produced the sixty-six books of the Bible. These books contained information their writers couldn't have known and concepts they couldn't have begun to imagine apart from supernatural inspiration.

And, even more thrilling for a scientist, the books of the Old and New Testaments made statements and predictions that could be tested. They literally invite testing! Deuteronomy 18:21–22 encourages readers to disregard any message given by someone who claims to speak for God if that message is not totally accurate. The New Testament book of 1 Corinthians says that if Jesus of Nazareth did not actually rise from the dead (as confirmed by eyewitness accounts), then any preaching or faith concerning him is in vain (see 1 Cor. 15:12–14).

The apostle Paul clarified this careful approach in his first letter to the Thessalonians: "Test everything. Hold on to the good" (1 Thess. 5:21). The Bible calls for an exploration of the truth with eyes wide open and mind engaged. Permitting scientific and spiritual curiosity to work together sets people free to run toward, not away from, the complex *why* questions.

To Address Complaints and Concerns

Between the ages of seven and nine, I read as many books as I could on astronomy and the history of astronomy. During my teenage years I was surprised to learn that the objections to a "created" universe raised in centuries past were the opposite of those being voiced in the twentieth century.

About Size

Previous to the twentieth century and the building of telescopes that can clearly see galaxies beyond the outer limits of the Milky Way, scientists and philosophers tended to complain that the universe was far too small to be the work of God. While acknowledging that the existence of the universe implied some kind of cosmic Creator, these researchers deduced that the Creator could not be very big or strong. If God were all-powerful and infinite, surely, they reasoned, he would have created an infinite universe or at least a much larger universe.[2] These concerns raised doubt about the existence of a biblical cosmic Creator.

The arrival of the twenty-first century and telescopes powerful enough to help us see back in time (see "Looking Back in Time," p. 21), even as far back as the initial moments of cosmic existence, has prompted a very different kind of complaint from scientists and skeptics. The universe as now measured appears absurdly too large to serve merely as humanity's home. Skeptics insist that a Creator, especially the biblical Creator, wouldn't make unnecessary matter and space or waste creative effort.

Historically, the same type of back-and-forth dissatisfaction has been expressed about Earth's size. In the fifteenth and sixteenth

Looking Back in Time

Because light takes time to travel through space, astronomers never witness the present. They only measure the past. For example, when astronomers observe the Sun, they see it not as it is now but rather as it was about eight minutes and twenty seconds ago (the amount of time required for light to travel from the Sun to Earth). Likewise, because the Andromeda Galaxy lies 2.1 million light-years away, we see what was happening in the Andromeda Galaxy 2.1 million years ago (see figure 1.1).

Figure 1.1. The Andromeda Galaxy as It Appeared Long Ago

This image reveals what the Andromeda Galaxy looked like 2.1 million years ago. Since then, the dwarf galaxy situated above and slightly to the left of the nucleus of Andromeda has moved even farther away from the nucleus. Its movement has contributed to the warping of Andromeda's spiral arms. Between the epoch captured by this photo and today, about 40,000 supernova eruptions have occurred and to some degree altered the Andromeda Galaxy in ways that cannot yet be seen. (Image courtesy of Corbis)

Thanks to modern technology, astronomers today have access to images that show what was taking place in the universe many billions of years ago. Several independent measures establish with a high degree of certainty that the universe is, indeed, 13.73 billion years old. Astronomical images now cover the entire span of cosmic history. In other words, astronomers can directly observe all of cosmic history from its beginning until the present.

Such observational capability explains why some of the most compelling scientific evidences for the existence and attributes of the Creator arise from the discipline of astronomy.[3] (If you are concerned that a universe billions of years old may be incompatible with a literal interpretation of the Bible, see appendix A: Biblical Basis for an Ancient Universe and Earth, p. 207.)

centuries, explorers, merchants, and kings expressed displeasure that India and Indonesia were so distant from Europe. Surely an all-loving, all-caring God could have blessed humanity with a small enough planet to make for more convenient trade routes.

Today people complain that Earth provides humanity with too little living space. They claim that an all-loving, all-caring God would not have confined humanity to the surface of a few continental landmasses on a relatively small planet. The thought that God would taunt humanity with the vastness of the cosmos and an impulse to colonize, while at the same time shackling us with physical laws and dimensions that deny any realistic capacity to spread our peoples and civilization to other bodies throughout the universe, seems mean-spirited.[4]

These grievances about the size of the universe and of Earth may say more about the arrogance of humanity than about the deficiencies of the Creator. Chapters 2 and 7 tackle the good reasons, as currently understood, for the vastness of the universe and the minuteness of humanity's habitat.

About Age

People also wonder or grumble about the age of the universe. Now that astronomers have determined the universe's age to be 13.73 billion years, many scholars and laypeople ask why, if God's goal in creating the universe was to provide a home for humanity, he took so much time. They suggest that an all-powerful God would have set up everything all at once (or simultaneously).[5] Even a weak God should have been able to prepare us a place in much less time than billions of years. Chapter 3 examines the question of why the universe must be so very ancient. Chapter 6 considers why the time window for the duration of human civilization, even in a vastly ancient cosmos, must be relatively brief.

About Loneliness

One summer while a graduate student at the University of Toronto, I had the privilege of taking a short course from Carl Sagan. He spoke about the unimaginable loneliness of this vast cosmos *if* indeed humans are the only intelligent species residing within it. Surely, Sagan reasoned, given the enormous size of the universe and Earth's capacity to support human life, billions of other astronomical bodies must also be endowed with the ability to support physical intelligent life.

Could there be sound reasons for believing we are isolated? More than thirty years after Sagan's speculations, the scientific discoveries discussed in chapter 4 illustrate the likelihood that we are isolated. Chapter 8 examines why physical intelligent life demands a unique planet, moon, star, set of planets, galaxy, and cluster of galaxies. In addition, it supplies observational evidence to support this uniqueness.

About Darkness

One of the most remarkable sets of scientific discoveries of the past decade is the recognition by astronomers that 99.73 percent of everything that exists in the universe is "dark" (see table 2.1, p. 37). These discoveries raise the obvious question of why a created universe would be such a dark place.

In addition to the universe as a whole being dark, astronomers have found that Earth resides in the darkest location within the Milky Way Galaxy where physical life is possible. And our Milky Way Galaxy lies in the darkest location in the universe where physical life is possible. Why? Chapter 5 grapples with the answers to each of these questions.

About Evil

The most serious complaints about the structure of the universe focus on the fact that the cosmos permits suffering, hardship, and evil. From many people's perspective, life appears *too* hard and *too* painful. Both humans and animals appear to suffer more than kindness would allow.

Who among us hasn't asked why an all-powerful, all-wise, and all-loving Creator would have designed a universe so full of horrors and heartaches? Surely such a Creator could have designed the cosmos so people and animals could live in comfort and peace.

Some say all this suffering seems gratuitous, pointless, even sadistic. The skeptic concludes that if God really knew what he was doing when he created the universe, he would have designed humanity's home so that tragedies couldn't happen or, at the very least, so humans would be protected from exposure to evil.

Could any type of pain, calamity, or exposure to evil be considered in some way *good*? Chapters 6–7 and 9–12 provide intriguing insights about the role of hardships and evil as experienced by all living beings. These chapters demonstrate how the present universe is ideally suited for bringing about an efficient and rapid end to all such suffering forever. They also make a case for defining *perfection* in the context of humanity's ultimate purpose and destiny.

About God's Obscurity

Why do so many people who study the universe find it difficult to see God or at least recognize his actions in shaping creation? Couldn't he have made it much easier for humans to see his glory and goodness in the heavens? Does he have to be "invisible," hidden from objective investigations? Chapter 10 focuses on why the universe might seem spiritually opaque and how, thanks to some new discoveries, God's revelation of himself now manifests more remarkable clarity than ever.

About Life's Mysteries

Perhaps the greatest question about life is why it has to end. Death seems so grievous, final, and unfair—not to mention so painful for those who survive. It appears to defy any concept of a caring and loving Creator. Why people must die, why animals die, why there were billions of years of death before humanity came on the scene, and what possible good could come from all this death are the subjects of chapters 6–7 and 10–11. These chapters also address the question of when and why the universe must come to an end.

Chapter 13 draws from various biblical passages to sketch a picture of the *new* creation, the "universe" yet to come. A glimpse into the future helps make sense of our yearnings for what this current cosmos does not provide.

To Embrace the Incomprehensible

Why is the universe so hugely vast, so unimaginably ancient, so predominantly dark, so irreversibly decaying, so empty of life, and so rife with suffering and evil? These questions deserve thoughtful responses. Many people wonder, as I once did, whether satisfying answers can be found.

As recently as a few decades ago, questions like these were thought to reside mostly in the domain of theology and philosophy. No one denies that these dilemmas are deeply philosophical and theological in nature, and yet scientific findings play a valuable role in either confirming or denying any proposed solutions. China's distinguished astrophysicist Fang Li Zhi declares, "A question that has always been considered a topic of metaphysics or theology—the creation of the universe—has now become an area of active research in physics."[6] Leading-edge research has opened the way for scientists to add their voices to the discussion of why the universe is the way it is.

Understanding the totality of the Creator's purposes for the universe will always remain beyond the reach of human minds. Even Hawking, with all his brilliance and zeal to discover "nothing less than a complete description of the universe we live in"[7] and "a complete *understanding* of the events around us, and of our own existence"[8] and to "know the mind of God,"[9] cannot realistically accomplish such a task.

I can say with reasonable certainty that humans are not God, nor can we become God. No mere human can know absolutely everything about *any* aspect of the cosmos because people are confined to a limited portion of the universe's space-time continuum. Thus, to gain a complete description and understanding of the universe is impossible. However, such limitations don't prevent those with curiosity from gathering adequate descriptions and understandings.

Many people, including myself, find contentment in "sufficient" answers, answers that become more complete over time, that challenge us to dig deeper and discover more of what *can* be known about the universe and humanity's place within it. I think that's what we all really want—to know *enough* to find satisfaction and make wise decisions.

And I'm firmly convinced we can know enough. Not enough to end all questions, but enough to make sense of our lives. We can build a cosmic perspective solid enough to remain firm yet flexible enough to absorb the impact of new discoveries.

Discovering the hidden purposes of creation can bring more than just a little contentment. Exploring why the universe is the way it is can help us develop a renewed sense of appreciation for the value of this life, an assurance of individual worth and eternal destiny, and an eager anticipation for what lies ahead.

Finding out why the universe is so huge seems a good place to begin.

2

Why Such a Vast Universe?

The sheer enormity of the universe is enough to make anyone feel inconsequential. This feeling raises questions: Does life really have any ultimate value, meaning, or purpose? If God is responsible for our existence, why would the universe be so large?

Although skeptics once argued that the universe was too small (see chapter 1, p. 20), today they charge that it's much too large to befit a divine Creator. They presume, "If God's goal was to make a habitat for humanity, he would not have made so many useless galaxies, stars, planets, comets, elements, and other components."

Physicist Victor Stenger states the skeptic's case:

> If God created the universe as a special place for humanity, he seems to have wasted an awfully large amount of space where humanity will never make an appearance.[1]

Stephen Hawking echoes this concern:

> Our Solar System is certainly a prerequisite for our existence. . . . But there does not seem to be any need for all these other galaxies.[2]

Stenger also points out that only a tiny fraction (0.0007) of the mass of the universe is carbon. "Yet," he questions, "we are supposed to think that God specially designed the universe so it would have the ability to manufacture in stars the carbon needed for life?"[3] (See "Why So Little Carbon?") He claims, "Energy is wasted, too. Of all the energy emitted by the sun, only two photons in a billion are used to warm Earth, the rest radiating uselessly into space."[4]

Few people can relate to what astronomers and physicists face every day—their measurements of how vast, massive, energetic, and ancient the universe really is. Its features, including its enormity, are virtually impossible to visualize. Perhaps imagining the cosmos as a vehicle—say, a car—can help.

Like an automobile, the universe:

1. has a mass density that can be measured,
2. appears to have been manufactured to certain specifications,
3. carries passengers,
4. burns fuel and emits exhaust,

Why So Little Carbon?

Without carbon, physical life is impossible. No other element displays the rich chemical behavior needed to form the range of complex molecular structures life requires. Given that physical life must be carbon-based, why would God make a universe with so little carbon?

Researchers have found that the quantity of carbon must be carefully balanced between just enough and not too much because carbon, though essential for life, can also be destructive to life. Too much carbon translates into too much carbon dioxide, carbon monoxide, and methane. In large quantities, these gases are poisonous. In modest quantities, their greenhouse properties keep the planet sufficiently warm for life. In larger quantities, they can heat a planet's surface beyond what physical life can tolerate.

One of the wonders of Earth is that it is sufficiently carbon-rich *and* carbon-poor. It carries enough carbon for life but not so much as to interfere with life's atmospheric needs, such as the appropriate pressure and density for efficient operation of lungs and a temperature range (and variability) that supports a wide diversity of active, advanced species.

---

5. moves forward (though it cannot reverse),
6. is capable of slowing down and speeding up (though not of standing still),
7. won't run forever.

This analogy is far from perfect, but no illustration is. For that matter, neither is any car. I'm reminded of that fact whenever I detect a ping in my engine or notice a puddle of some colorful liquid on my garage floor. I'm reminded again as I turn into the parking lot most weekdays at Reasons To Believe (RTB).

No two cars there are exactly alike because no particular make or model meets everyone's transportation needs, preferences, and budget. Dave, Bob, Esther, Patti, Michelle, Scott, Diana, Phil, and the rest of the RTB staff chose their wheels based on the principle of optimization—what's best for each of them, all things considered. By contrast the universe is optimized for every human being—a one-year make-and-model best suited for fulfillment of *all* God's purposes. See more on this topic of optimization in chapters ahead. For the moment, the visibility factor illustrates the point.

Visibility

One of the great wonders of the universe is an amazing gift that most people take for granted: the ability to see into the distance. Clarity makes an astounding difference when it comes to exploring, measuring, and understanding the cosmos. The more astronomers learn about the universe, the more they recognize how remarkable it is that *the multiple cosmic characteristics that make human life possible also make the universe visible, knowable, and measurable.*

If the universe were any smaller or larger, younger or older, brighter or darker, more or less efficient as a radiator, and if human observers were located where most stars and planets reside, the view would be so blocked as to give few (if any) clues about what lies beyond. We would be blind to the realm we live in!

More importantly, no one would even be around to see it. Chapters 3 and 5 explain in detail how the visibility and measurability of the universe from humanity's specific time window and from Earth's specific location are, by themselves, indicators of a Creator with a purpose for both the cosmos and humanity.

Super-Sized

Fortunately, humans are present to take advantage of a rare moment in cosmic history and an ideal location in cosmic geography from which to gaze out over the vast expanse of the universe. As a result, scientists can uncover its secrets. But why would the universe need to be so big if just one relatively tiny planet with its population of humans is the focal point of God's creation? Why all the rest of this stuff? Exactly how much of it can be accounted for?

Until recently astronomers had no accurate measure of the number of stars and galaxies in the observable universe (see "Difference between the Observable and the Actual Universe,"). But

---

Difference between the Observable and the Actual Universe

The universe that exists today is different from the universe that astronomers actually observe. Astronomers look *back* in time when they look at distant objects because light (even though it's very fast moving) takes time to travel through space. Thus, the universe astronomers observe is the universe of the past. The farther away astronomers look, the farther back in time they see. So, for example, when astronomers produce an image of a cluster of galaxies two billion light-years away, that image shows them what the cluster of galaxies was like two billion years ago.

In a continuously expanding universe, the universe of the past is spatially smaller than the universe of the present. And more stars form as it continues to expand. Therefore, the observable universe is spatially smaller and contains fewer stars than the actual universe. (Note that all the matter and energy of the universe, including the stars and galaxies, are confined to the surface of the universe.) How much smaller depends on the geometry of the space-time surface of the universe. While the geometry of the universe isn't yet known with the degree of accuracy astronomers hope to acquire, astronomers do know that the actual universe of the present must be at least an order of magnitude (a factor of ten) larger than the universe they observe via telescopes.

this situation changed in 2005, when scientists aimed the Hubble Space Telescope at a little patch of sky no bigger than one-tenth of the Moon's diameter. Astronomers collected light from this region for a million seconds (278 hours), the longest exposure ever taken by any telescopic "camera." With an exceptionally deep look into the heavens, labeled the Hubble Ultra Deep Field, astronomers successfully imaged all the galaxies (or at least all the larger-than-dwarf galaxies) that could possibly reside in the region—including the very first galaxies that formed in the universe.[5]

The Hubble Ultra Deep Field (see figure 2.1, p. 32) showed astronomers slightly more than 10,000 galaxies. Given the observed uniformity of the cosmos on large-distance scales (which is a fundamental requirement for life in the universe[6]), researchers could then do the math: more than 10,000 galaxies multiplied over the whole area of the sky totaled 200 billion galaxies in the observable universe. These 200 billion galaxies contain, on average, about 200 billion stars each. So the total number of stars in these galaxies adds up to about 40 billion trillion—and that's without the estimated 10 billion trillion stars contained in the unobserved dwarf galaxies. Somewhere around 50 billion trillion stars make their home in the observable universe.

That's a mind-boggling number. A comparison may make it more comprehensible: if that same number of dimes were packed together as densely as possible and piled 1,500 feet high (as high as some of the world's tallest skyscrapers), they would cover the entire North American continent.

Here's another attempt at comparison. Shrink an average star (about a million miles in diameter) down to the size of a grapefruit. Hold that grapefruit and ask a friend to hold another. Given the average distance between stars in the Milky Way Galaxy (about forty trillion miles), can you guess where your friend would have to take her grapefruit to illustrate the distance between stars? If you, with grapefruit in hand, stood in downtown Los Angeles, she would have to travel to Peru or Siberia. Now try to imagine that distance multiplied 40 million times (that's the necessary diameter of a volume large enough to accommodate 50 billion trillion grapefruits). Given all the empty space between galaxies, the universe

Figure 2.1. The Hubble Ultra Deep Field

This image produced by the Hubble Space Telescope is the deepest cosmic penetration ever achieved by an optical telescope. Every spot or smudge depicts a galaxy—except for the few foreground stars identifiable by crosslike optical defects. Some of these galaxies are over 13 billion light-years away. At this distance, they must be among the first galaxies ever to form in the history of the universe. (Image courtesy of NASA and the Hubble Space Telescope Institute)

on this stars-as-grapefruits scale would actually be much bigger than this calculated diameter!

The Matter of Mass

Volume gives one indication of the universe's enormity. Mass density gives another. For example, the cars in RTB's parking lot can be sized up by their dimensions (volume) *or* by their weight (more accurately referred to as mass). Two of the biggest cars in our lot are Fuz's Ford station wagon and Phil's Mercedes sedan (obviously he worked at a for-profit company before joining the ministry staff). Fuz's car is "vast" in terms of length, width, and height. Phil's car, on the other hand, is smaller in size but more "vast" in terms of mass density (weight per volume, roughly). In a collision with a semi, Phil's car would likely fare better than Fuz's because it weighs more.

The universe is much larger than its observable volume, more vast than its observable number of stars and galaxies would indicate (see "Difference between the Observable and the Actual Universe," p. 30). What's more, the totality of its stars—those seen, those unseen, and those long-ago burned out—account for just 1 percent of the universe's total mass.[7] No wonder some people consider this incredible enormity a "waste" if humans are the main focus of the universe's existence. However, if humans are to exist, this enormous mass is critical.

Right Mass, Right Elements

Anyone who hasn't had the privilege of studying astrophysics may not realize that the universe *must* be as massive as it is or human life would not be possible—for at least two reasons. The first concerns the production of life-essential elements.

The density of protons and neutrons in the universe relates to the cosmic mass, or mass density. That density determines how much hydrogen, the lightest of the elements, fuses into heavier elements during the first few minutes of cosmic existence. And the amount of heavier elements determines how much additional heavy-element production occurs later in the nuclear furnaces of stars.

If the density of protons and neutrons were significantly lower (than enough to convert about 1 percent of the universe's mass into stars), then nuclear fusion would proceed less efficiently. As a result, the cosmos would never be capable of generating elements heavier than helium—elements like carbon, nitrogen, oxygen, phosphorus, sodium, and potassium, which are essential for any kind of physical life. On the other hand, if the density of protons and neutrons were slightly higher (enough to convert significantly more than 1 percent of the mass of the universe into stars), nuclear fusion would be too productive. All the hydrogen in the universe would rapidly fuse into elements as heavy as, or heavier than, iron. Again, life-essential elements (carbon, nitrogen, oxygen, etc.), including hydrogen, would not exist.

Right Mass, Right Expansion Rate

The second reason the universe must be hugely massive concerns its expansion rate. The rate at which the universe expands throughout cosmic history critically depends on its mass density. According to the law of gravity, the closer any two massive bodies are to one another, the more powerfully those bodies attract each other. Therefore, the closer various bits and pieces of mass are to one another in the universe, the more effectively they will slow down the universe's expansion. Conversely, the farther apart those bits and pieces are, the less "braking effect" gravity has on cosmic expansion.

Without any additional cosmic density factors such as dark energy (see pp. 38–40), a universe with less mass density would not form stars like the Sun and planets like Earth. Its expansion would be so rapid that gravity would not have opportunity to pull together the gas and dust to make such bodies. Yet if the cosmic mass density were any greater, gas and dust would condense so effectively under gravity's influence that all stars would be much larger than the Sun. Any planets such stars might hold in their orbit would be unsuitable for life because of the intensity of the stars' radiation and because of rapid changes in the stars' temperature, radiation, and luminosity—not to mention the radiation and gravitational disturbances caused by neighboring supergiant stars.

With only a little extra mass, the universe would expand so slowly that all stars in the cosmos would rapidly become black holes and neutron stars. The density near the surface of such bodies would exceed five billion tons per teaspoon (one billion tons per cubic centimeter). At such enormous densities, molecules are impossible. So are atoms. Therefore, life would be impossible.

The radiation and gravitational disturbances from such black holes and neutron stars would also make physical life impossible anywhere in such a dense universe. Physical life cannot exist in a universe with a mass density any less or any more than the actual cosmic value.

Some might argue that a sheer coincidence explains the particular mass density of the universe and, therefore, that the universe's mass implies nothing about intentionality. However, the mass of the universe is fine-tuned to provide two life-essential features simultaneously: (1) the just-right amounts and diversity of elements, and (2) the just-right expansion rates throughout cosmic history so that certain types of stars and planets form at the just-right times and in the just-right locations. Fine-tuning to provide two life-essential characteristics at once hints louder than a whisper at purposeful design. So does the high degree of fine-tuning.

An Exquisite Balance

While stars and planets account for only about 1 percent of the total matter (hence mass) of the universe, even that small percentage must be extraordinarily fine-tuned for life to exist. Picture a huge vehicle—something much bigger than a car. Maybe the U.S. Navy's aircraft carrier the USS *John C. Stennis* (see figure 2.2, p. 36). Now imagine a tiny fleck of paint from that ship, so small against your hand you can barely see it. If such a vehicle were compared to the universe in its earliest moments, removing that speck or adding an extra drop of paint to it would be enough to alter the vehicle's mass so much as to make it completely useless for transporting passengers.

In reality, the delicacy of that ratio is far more extreme than the ship analogy reveals. For the reasons noted above, and *if* no other density factors influence the expansion of the universe (see pp. 38–40), at certain early epochs in cosmic history, its mass density must have been as finely tuned as one part in 10^{60} to allow for the possible existence of physical life at any time or place within the entirety of the universe.[8] This degree of fine-tuning is so great that it's as if right after the universe's beginning someone could have destroyed the possibility of life within it by subtracting a single dime's mass from the whole of the observable universe or adding a single dime's mass to it. (See appendix B, pp. 209–11.)

Figure 2.2. The USS *John C. Stennis*

This United States Navy aircraft carrier is 1,092 feet long. A self-contained city, it has a displacement of 100,000 tons when fully loaded. If the USS *John C. Stennis* were as fine-tuned as the universe, adding or subtracting a billionth of a trillionth of the mass of an electron from the total mass of the aircraft carrier would make it uninhabitable. (Courtesy of the United States Navy. Photo taken by U.S. Navy Mass Communication Specialist 3rd Class Paul J. Perkins)

Recently astronomers have discovered evidence that other cosmic density factors *do*, in fact, influence cosmic expansion (see table 2.1, p. 37). These factors, while reducing the degree of fine-tuning in the cosmic mass density, introduce far more spectacular fine-tuning elsewhere (see pp. 209–11). The illustration of adding or subtracting a dime's mass to the universe is too conservative. The fine-tuning of the cosmic density parameters is far more impressive (see the discussion and sidebar on pp. 38–40 and appendix B).

Dark Matter

In addition to a specific cosmic mass, with quantities of protons and neutrons precisely fixed to make life possible, astronomers now recognize that every component that makes up the universe,

TABLE 2.1

Inventory of All the Stuff That Makes Up the Universe

Cosmic component	Percentage of total cosmic density
Dark energy (self-stretching property of the cosmic space surface)	72.1
Exotic dark matter (particles that weakly interact with ordinary matter particles and light)	23.3
Ordinary dark matter (particles that strongly interact with light)	4.35
Ordinary bright matter (stars and star remnants)	0.27
Planets (a subset of ordinary dark matter)	0.0001

Note: This inventory began with an exhaustive compilation by Princeton cosmologists Masataka Fukugita and James Peebles. It was based initially on the best measurements prior to 2005.[9] Updates were made possible in 2006 and 2008 by the second and third releases of the Wilkinson Microwave Anisotropy Probe's (WMAP) results.[10]

both matter and nonmatter, must be present at a specified value or physical life would not exist.

Little more than half a century ago astronomers came to realize that the stuff they see through their telescopes makes up only a tiny fraction of the total amount of matter in the universe.[11] As that realization dawned, astronomers hypothesized that this "dark matter" was made up of cold gas and failed stars[12] ("brown dwarfs," stars with so little mass they never ignite nuclear fusion[13]). When it became apparent that the maximum contribution from cold gas and failed stars was grossly inadequate to account for the total, Princeton University astronomer James Peebles proposed that the dark matter was composed of small rocks. Peebles's proposal led to a familiar joke among astronomers that "the universe either was Peebled with pebbles or pebbled with Peebles." Ongoing research has led to the development of an inventory, a list of the various components that comprise the universe—both matter and energy (see table 2.1).

After acknowledging that the total quantity of protons and neutrons in the universe must be set at a precise value for the universe to produce the right kinds and quantities of life-essential elements at the right times in cosmic history, astronomers discovered yet another fine-tuned feature. The proportion of ordinary bright matter (the protons and neutrons that form stars) with relation to ordinary dark matter (the protons and neutrons that form gas, dust, rocks, and planets) must also be fine-tuned for life. Too much or too little of the bright stuff would expose potential life-forms to either too much or too little light, heat, and radiation, for example. The abundance of life-essential elements and of radioactive isotopes is also affected by this balance. As it turns out, life requires that 5 percent of ordinary matter be bright and 95 percent dark.

But ordinary matter does not add up to enough mass to generate the required expansion history of the universe. This history must be just right, with the universe expanding at the just-right rates at the just-right times, for life to be possible. Some other form of matter must have been available in a precise abundance and location. Theorists calculated that this other matter, now called exotic matter (comprised of particles that interact only weakly, if at all, with ordinary matter particles and light), would need to be nearly five times more abundant than the ordinary matter, for life's sake. And that's what researchers have found.

In other words, not only must the universe be as massive and vast as it is (given the cosmic mass density and expansion time required to make a planet like Earth), but also each of the different mass components must be neither smaller nor larger than they are. (Additional fine-tuning requirements for the quantities and the locations of the different forms of matter are addressed in chapter 3.) However, not all of what makes up the universe is matter.

Dark Energy

Much in the same manner as a car, the universe has separate systems for slowing down and speeding up. Gravity functions as the main braking system. During the early era of the universe, before its mass became widely dispersed, gravity effectively applied the brakes on the universe, slowing down its expansion from its initial creative burst. This creation event is familiarly referred to as the big bang.

A bizarre feature called "dark energy" (discovered so recently that the scientific community still hasn't settled on exactly what to call it) serves as the acceleration system. Perhaps this quality is best described as a self-stretching property of the cosmic surface (the spatial surface of the universe along which all matter and energy are distributed). For the first approximately 7 billion years of its existence, the universe expanded at a decelerating rate. Then, as the components of the universe gradually spread apart, gravity became progressively weaker in its capacity to slow down the expansion, and dark energy gradually became stronger or more effective in its capacity to accelerate the expansion. This dark energy effect may be described as a self-stretching capacity that increases as the surface of the universe continues to expand (see "What Is Dark Energy?" p. 40).

Eventually dark energy's accelerating effect overtook the braking effect of gravity, and for approximately the last 6.7 billion years cosmic expansion has been speeding up.[14] In the future, the effect of gravity will become increasingly weaker in its capacity to slow down cosmic expansion while the effect of dark energy (assuming no radical alteration in its future behavior) will grow increasingly stronger. As a result the universe will continue to expand at an accelerating rate.

The observational verifications that dark energy is the predominant component of the universe and, therefore, that the universe will expand at an ever-increasing rate put an effectual end to the oscillating universe model and to the Hindu/Buddhist concept of a reincarnating universe.[15] Accelerating cosmic expansion means the universe can never contract; therefore it cannot rebound. This fact eliminates the possibility of a renewal, rebirth, or second beginning for the universe. The natural consequences for life in a universe that can die (from a "heat death" caused by continuing expansion making the universe colder and colder) but can never be "reborn" are addressed in chapter 6.

Much in the same way as the mass density of the universe must be fine-tuned to ensure that the universe expands in exactly the way life requires, the dark energy density also must be exquisitely fine-tuned. However, its fine-tuning is orders of magnitude more stringent. If dark energy were changed by as little as one part in

---

What Is Dark Energy?

Though often described in popular literature as an antigravity force, dark energy is not a force. A better, though still imperfect, analogy would be to describe it as the opposite of the effect you feel when stretching an elastic band.

The more an elastic band is stretched, the more energy it gains to encourage its contraction. Thus, the more someone stretches the band with his fingers, the more he feels the tension that impels the band to contract.

The surface of the universe acts the opposite way—it is like a gigantic elastic band that *wants* to expand outward. The more the cosmic surface stretches, the more energy the surface gains to propel even more stretching of the surface. When the universe was very young, gravity kept it from expanding much more rapidly from its initial infinitesimally small volume. At that time, dark energy would have been relatively weak in its capacity to expand or stretch out the space surface of the universe.

However, as the universe grew older and older, the cosmic space surface became bigger and bigger. This increasing size of the cosmic surface meant much more dark energy became available to expand the cosmic space surface.

Thus the entirety of the universe eventually began to expand at an accelerating rate. That's because all of the universe's matter and energy, as well as its space-time dimensions, are confined to its surface.

Astronomers have yet to determine the nature of dark energy precisely enough to make a confident pronouncement. It is even possible, though not probable, that two or three factors contribute to the dark energy effect. The latest studies favor a single factor. They reveal that the dark energy density is roughly constant throughout cosmic history, or at least all but its earliest moments.[16]

10^{120}, the universe would be unable to support life.[17] A number that small can be hard to picture. If compared to the mass of the entire universe, it would be no bigger than a billionth of a trillionth of a trillionth of an electron's mass. (For additional details, see appendix B, "Where Is the Cosmic Density Fine-Tuning?")

Clear and Present Purposes

Both cosmic mass density and dark energy density hugely impact not only the possibility for human life but also the possibility for individuals to observe, explore, and understand the universe. Given the particular laws and constants of physics that govern the universe, the possibility for life and discovery mandate that the universe be vast in all ways, including volume and mass, at the particular epoch during which intelligent life exists.

The skeptic might say it's conceivable, though not necessarily possible, that a different set of laws, constants, and dimensions might provide humanity with an acceptable habitat without requiring such an incredibly vast universe. The following chapters address that challenge from the perspective of purposes beyond mere provision of a habitable environment. These additional purposes are reflected in the specific set of physical laws, constants, and dimensions the universe manifests. Given this unique set, the universe must indeed be as vast and as massive as it is.

And though its enormity strains the human capability to imagine, that vastness says something about the high value of and high purposes for humanity's existence. Rather than seeing ourselves as insignificant specks in the immensity of the cosmos, we can consider that immensity an indicator of our worth. It seems the Creator invested a great deal—a universe of 50 billion trillion stars, plus a hundred times more matter, all fine-tuned to mind-boggling precision—for us. If not for the strength and abundance of evidence in support of that notion, it would seem the height of arrogance. Humility demands that we take a deeper and wider look at that evidence.

Chapter 5 discusses the significance of cosmic darkness. Chapters 6–7 and 10–12 explain the role of physical laws and constants. But first let's consider the topic of the universe's immense age and how it reveals more hidden purposes.

3

Why Such an Old Universe?

When my older son was just a toddler, he heard from a local librarian that the universe of stars and space is "without beginning or end." That week's story time was a bit out of date from a scientific perspective.

This same librarian would have laughed if she'd read a story saying that cars have always existed and always will. Abundant historical records include photographs that depict the origin and history of the automobile. And anyone who cares to study them can.

Though I'm not all that familiar with cars, I've learned enough to recognize which cars in RTB's parking lot are "vintage" vehicles. Based on their features (more than on their wear and tear), I can even estimate when they were made. Diana's sleek metallic bronze Cougar dates to the 1970s, and Michelle's boxy slate blue Falcon wagon dates back to the 1960s.

Just as we can see well-preserved models and photos of cars from throughout their history, so too scientists can use available technology to see the universe throughout its history. Over the past few decades, astronomers have been building a record that includes graphic images. Even people with little scientific education can see how the universe looked at various stages along the way, from the beginning onward.

The chronological sequence of those images reveals multiple signs of advancing age. It also shows why the universe must have reached certain milestones before humans could exist and thrive. It can be neither younger nor older to best suit our needs.

Amazing new instruments allow astronomers to observe and measure the radiation still left from the event that brought the cosmos into being. One set of images shows that moment when darkness first separated from light—soon after all the matter, energy, space, and time known as the universe came into existence from a reality beyond the cosmos.

Just-Right Age to Support Humanity

While cars have only been on the scene for a little more than 100 years, the latest measurements indicate the universe has been around for 13.73 billion years.[1] That may seem like a long time from a layperson's perspective, but astronomers think otherwise. From an astronomical view, 13.73 billion years represents the minimum time necessary to prepare a home for humanity. And as it turns out, the minimum time required is essentially the same as the maximum time for at least three reasons:

1. Essential heavy elements need to build up.

For its first 365 million years, the universe contained only five elements: hydrogen, helium, and tiny traces of lithium, beryllium, and boron. In addition to hydrogen and (in the case of plants) boron, life requires over twenty different elements heavier than boron. These elements include carbon, nitrogen, oxygen, phosphorous, potassium, calcium, and iron. But the big bang creation event yielded none of them.

Manufactured exclusively in the nuclear furnaces of stars, these elements built up gradually. The universe didn't contain the variety and concentrations of heavy elements necessary to make planets and advanced life possible until after three generations of stars formed, burned, and scattered their ashes into the interstellar medium.

Human civilization, including high-tech societies with auto-mobiles, demands a far greater variety and abundance of heavy elements and radioactive isotopes (see reason #2). Their creation took at least 9 billion years of heavy-element manufacture in stellar furnaces. That's how long it would have taken, at minimum, to provide for a heavy-metal-rich planet such as Earth. And slightly more than 4.5 billion years ago, just as that essential abundance first became available, Earth's solar system came together.

2. Long-lived radioactive isotopes need to build up.

As the universe ages and the abundance of heavy elements increases, one class of elements eventually begins to decrease. Radioactive elements, more specifically radiometric isotopes (see "Radiometric Isotopes"), start to decay as soon as they form. Different radiometric isotopes manifest different rates of decay. So, depending on how rapidly stars replenish supplies, radiometric isotopes with slow decay rates can build up while those with rapid decay rates start to disappear.

As the universe ages, ongoing cosmic expansion disperses its matter more widely. The greater the dispersal of gas and dust in the universe, the less efficiently stars form. More importantly, ongoing star development depletes the universe's reservoirs of gas and dust. With less gas and dust, fewer stars are made. So as the universe gets older, star formation gradually tapers off. And as this manufacture

Radiometric Isotopes

An element is defined by the number of protons that reside in its nucleus. For example, all nuclei that contain six protons are carbon. All that contain seven are nitrogen, and all that contain eight protons are oxygen. However, each element is made up of a suite of different isotopes—that is, nuclei with the same number of protons but with different numbers of neutrons.

Most elements are comprised of one or more stable isotopes (those that do not experience any radiometric decay) and several more isotopes that break down. For some elements, like uranium and thorium, no isotopes are stable. All their isotopes undergo radiometric decay.

of new stars slows down, the rate of star explosions—especially the major ones called supernovae—also slows down.

Supernovae produce all the universe's long-lasting radiometric isotopes, mainly uranium-235, uranium-238, and thorium-232. These isotopes decay over time into helium and lead-207, lead-206, and lead-208, respectively. Half of any given amount of a radioactive isotope decays during a specific time period called a half-life. The half-life for uranium-235 is 0.704 billion years; for uranium-238, 4.468 billion years; and for thorium-232, 14.1 billion years.

As the rate of supernova events steadily declines with the universe's advancing age, a time comes in cosmic history when the production of new supplies of uranium-235, uranium-238, and thorium-232 can no longer keep pace with decay. In other words, at some point the amount of long-lived radiometric isotopes reaches a peak and after that steadily declines. In some ways, the situation resembles the buildup and then decline of available fossil fuels on Earth (see chapter 7, p. 110).

Uranium-235, uranium-238, and thorium-232 may seem obscure, even dangerous, but they play a critical role in making Earth suitable for human habitation. The radiation they release provides nearly all the energy that drives and sustains plate tectonics.[2] And the energy produced by these elements also helps sustain Earth's magnetic field.[3]

Earth's continents and oceans coexist due to plate tectonics. Tectonic activity also helps compensate for the changing luminosity (brightness) of the Sun throughout its history.[4] And without Earth's strong, long-lasting magnetic field, the Sun's radiation would soon sputter away much of Earth's atmosphere and allow deadly showers of cosmic radiation to reach the planet's surface.

Given the importance of uranium and thorium in serving the needs of advanced life, the best possible time for an advanced-life-habitable planet to form would be when uranium and thorium reach their peak abundances. Recent research reveals that the timing of that peak occurred when the universe was two-thirds of its present age—about 4.57 billion years ago—or when the universe reached the tender age of about 9.2 billion years (see figure 3.1, p. 47). That age matches the timing of the Earth's formation 4.5662±0.0001 billion years ago.[5]

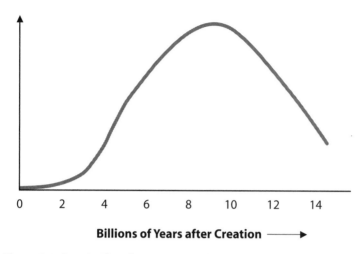

0 2 4 6 8 10 12 14

Billions of Years after Creation ⟶

Figure 3.1. Cosmic Abundance History of Uranium and Thorium

Supernovae deliver uranium and thorium to the interstellar medium. However, as the rate of supernova eruptions declines, a time comes when the amount delivered does not match the amount lost through radiometric decay. For Earth to be maximally supplied with uranium and thorium, the planet had to form during that time in cosmic history when the uranium and thorium abundance reached its peak. (Illustration by Jonathan Price)

3. Dangerous events must subside.

The same supernovae so crucial for building up the heavy elements and radiometric isotopes essential for advanced life also shower their environs with deadly radiation. Consequently, advanced life could not be safely introduced until the rate of supernova eruptions in the Milky Way Galaxy had subsided considerably. Bacterial life didn't need to wait so long, however, because it can survive under much harsher radiation conditions.[6]

Dense molecular clouds are another galactic hazard for advanced life. Fortunately, as the Milky Way Galaxy aged, ongoing star formation eventually consumed enough of the gas and dust in such clouds that they ceased to pose a major threat to advanced life.

Gamma-ray burst events, both in our galaxy and in nearby galaxies, pose an even deadlier risk to advanced life than supernovae or dense molecular clouds. But, like supernova eruption events, the rate of gamma-ray bursts subsided substantially once the universe exceeded the age of about 10 billion years.

Early collisions between the Milky Way Galaxy and other medium-sized galaxies during which the mass of the colliding galaxies merged would have seriously disrupted the structure of the Milky Way, making it uninhabitable for advanced life. Such galaxy-merging events were likely frequent during the Milky Way's youth, when the universe was more compressed and when the galaxy-merging process had not yet reduced the number of galaxies. Advanced life would not have survived our galaxy's youthful era.

Though a planet suitable for life's survival could be assembled within 9.2 billion years after the cosmic creation event, nearly another billion years would be required to prepare that planet for primitive life. Beyond that time, it took another 3.5 billion years for the supernova eruptions, dense molecular clouds, gamma-ray bursts, and galaxy-merging events—as well as other dangerous conditions—to subside enough for advanced life and civilization to survive and thrive.

Just-Right Terrestrial Age for Support of Humanity

The perfect time for a life-habitable solar system to form was about 9.2 billion years after the beginning of the universe—no sooner, no later. Cosmic reasons include those cited previously, but these aren't the only reasons. A number of terrestrial and solar system reasons account for the necessity of an additional 4.57-billion-year delay before the arrival of advanced life on the cosmic scene.

The Sun's Stability

As stars go, the Sun ranks as one of the most stable and benign stars we know of for the support of advanced life. Stars more massive than the Sun increase in brightness too quickly. Stars less massive manifest significantly greater flaring and chromospheric activity. However, all stars, including the Sun, exhibit some flaring activity. In the Sun's case, that flaring subsided to a minimum level when the Sun reached about 4.5 to 4.6 billion years of age (see figure 3.2).[7] So advanced life and civilization would not have been viable until then.

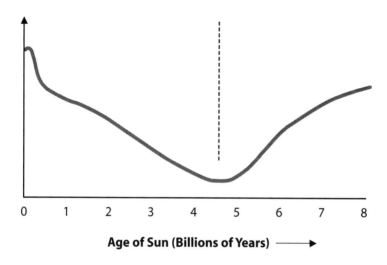

Age of Sun (Billions of Years) ⟶

Figure 3.2. Flaring Activity Level for the Sun

Only when the Sun was about halfway through its hydrogen-burning phase did its flare activity level become low enough not to pose a risk for humans or for advanced civilization. (Illustration by Jonathan Price)

The Sun's luminosity, or brightness, has changed significantly throughout its history. While young, the Sun dimmed for a while as it shed a small percentage of its mass to its environment (the interplanetary and interstellar media).[8] When the Sun grew older, it began to brighten as the conversion of hydrogen into helium in its nuclear furnace caused the furnace to burn hotter.[9] Given that humans and advanced civilization require a certain history of life's progression, including specific levels of diversity at specific times[10] and a certain minimum buildup of biodeposits, human arrival and survival on the terrestrial scene depended on the Sun's having reached a particular level of brightness (see figure 3.3, p. 50). This level was not reached until the Sun was about 4.5 to 4.6 billion years old.

The Bombardment Subsidence

During the solar system's youth, it was filled with an enormous abundance of asteroids, comets, rocks, and dust. This material

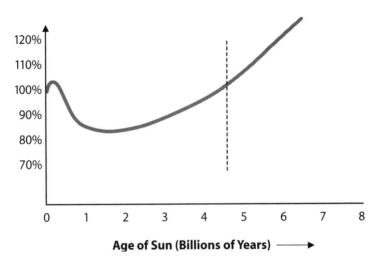

Figure 3.3. Luminosity History of the Sun

During the first billion to billion and a half years of the Sun's existence, it shed between 4 to 7 percent of its mass. This loss caused the Sun to dim by about 15 percent. Thereafter, the Sun's brightness steadily increased as more and more hydrogen in its core was converted into helium by the Sun's nuclear furnace. This extra amount of helium increased the core density of the Sun, which in turn caused the Sun's nuclear furnace to burn more efficiently. The more efficient nuclear furnace resulted in a progressively brighter Sun until it reached the brightness level required for global human civilization. (Illustration by Jonathan Price)

once pelted the Earth with great frequency and intensity. These bombardment events made the planet inhospitable to advanced life for a few billion years.

Bombardments also yielded some positive benefits for advanced life. They provided fresh supplies of water to replace that lost to outer space. They also salted Earth's surface with valuable mineral deposits. For example, the planet's richest nickel deposit, at Greater Sudbury in Ontario, Canada, is the result of an asteroid collision. For a few billion years, these deposits accrued for the maximum benefit of human civilization.

The Earth's Transformation

Advanced life on Earth needs a rotation rate very close to twenty-four hours per day. Tidal interaction with the Moon and Sun has steadily reduced Earth's rotation rate from its initial two or three hours per day down to its current twenty-four. However, it has taken about 4.5 billion years of tidal interaction to accomplish this reduction.

In addition, advanced life needs lots of free oxygen in its planetary atmosphere. For such oxygen to accumulate to the required level, a huge abundance of photosynthetic life had to work aggressively to pump out enough oxygen to fill oxygen sinks (oxygen-absorbing minerals) in both Earth's crust and mantle. Oxygen also had to reach appropriate levels in Earth's atmosphere. Figure 3.4 demonstrates how it took such life 3.8 billion years to raise the atmospheric oxygen level from less than 1 percent to its present 21 percent.[11]

For the human species to achieve a high population and high-technology global civilization, continental landmasses had to cover a significant fraction of the Earth's surface. Such coverage demanded the continual operation of plate tectonic activity

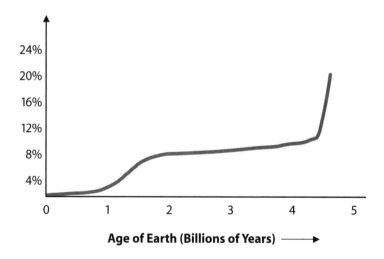

Age of Earth (Billions of Years) ⟶

Figure 3.4. Earth's Oxygenation History

The production of free oxygen by photosynthetic life over the past 3.8 billion years has augmented the level of oxygen in Earth's atmosphere from less than 1 percent to about 21 percent of Earth's total atmosphere. Until 205 million years ago, the level of oxygen in the atmosphere of the Earth never rose above 10 percent. (Illustration by Jonathan Price)

over a very long time. Figure 3.5 shows that more than four billion years of plate tectonics on Earth finally generated adequate continents and islands for the planet's human population and civilization.[12]

Many more reasons than these mandate that 4.5 to 4.6 billion years was the necessary preparation period before Earth was ready to receive the human species and its global civilization. Adding the 4.5–4.6 billion years of planetary history to the 9.2 billion years of cosmic history (required to form a planet endowed with the heavy elements and long-lived radioactive isotopes needed by advanced life) yields a required total cosmic age of 13.7 to 13.8 billion years. Given the laws of physics that govern the cosmos, the universe was ready to serve as a home for human beings at the earliest imaginable date. From an astrophysical perspective, its ancientness seems more like youth. (Reasons for its particular laws of physics are discussed in chapters 6, 8, 9, 11, and 12.)

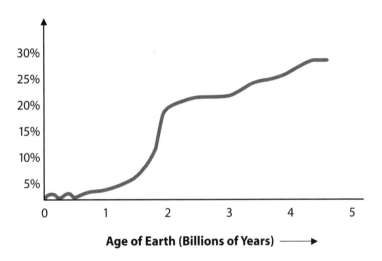

Figure 3.5. Growth of Continental Landmasses

Earth started off as a water world—a planet with water covering the whole of its surface. For the first billion years, small islands appeared and disappeared. Subsequently, aggressive plate tectonics caused continents to grow at a significantly faster rate than the rate at which erosion forces wore them down. Today, continents and islands cover 29 percent of the total surface area of Earth. (Illustration by Jonathan Price)

Just-Right Age for Observing

Besides needing nearly 14 billion years to build up all the resources necessary to make possible the existence of rocky planets, human beings, global civilization, and technology, there's another reason the universe must be that old. At 13.73 billion years of age, it is just old enough—and young enough—to facilitate its visual and technological exploration.

For several obvious and profound reasons, the universe must be that old for astronomers to properly study its history and structure. At least three of these reasons deserve examination.

First, in a continuously expanding universe, the space surface of a young universe would be much smaller than when the universe is older. A smaller space surface means that all the light-emitting objects in the cosmos—primarily stars, the regions around black holes, and galaxies—are jammed tightly together. The light of nearby objects would have blinded observers from seeing the more distant objects. Only in a universe where stars and galaxies are sufficiently spread apart can an observer potentially see everything the universe contains. It took billions of years for cosmic expansion to push the bright lights of the universe far enough apart for optimal visibility. (In the case of the Milky Way Galaxy, those bright lights are various galaxies in the Virgo supercluster.)

Second, these lights were much brighter in the past than they are today. The intensity of the light emitted by the cosmos is strongly tied to the rate of star formation. This rate reached a peak when the universe was about 5 to 6 billion years old. It took additional billions of years beyond that peak for the lights of the universe to dim sufficiently so as not to impair astronomers' viewing capacity.

Third, during Earth's infancy, its atmosphere was opaque to light. In its youth, the planet's atmosphere was translucent. Only when Earth reached what astronomers and physicists call "middle age" (an age of over 4 billion years) did its atmosphere become transparent enough to enable its inhabitants to observe the most distant objects in the universe. (While space-based telescopes are not limited by atmospheric image degradation and distortion, it is doubtful that humans ever would have placed such instruments in orbit without prior knowledge of the potential to gain significant information.)

Scientists gained profound understanding when they discovered that the laws and constants of physics themselves impose theoretical limits on how much cosmic history astronomers can view. Astronomers now recognize that only one relatively brief epoch in cosmic history allows for direct observation and measurement of its entire sweep.

For example, it takes time for light to travel from distant galaxies to an observer's telescope. Up to a certain limit, the older the universe, the greater the distance at which astronomers can make observations, or the farther back in time they can see. The universe is now sufficiently ancient that astronomers can actually witness the moment when light first separated from darkness (see figure 3.6).

The human era is theoretically the earliest possible epoch that allows astronomers to study the light from the origin of the universe. They can see that light clear back to 0.000028 of its present age. Because of the universe's age, astronomers can directly view 99.9972 percent of cosmic history and *almost* behold the instant of cosmic creation. Astronomers' analyses of maps of the radiation

Figure 3.6. When Light First Separated from Darkness

This map, from the third data release of the Wilkinson Microwave Anisotropy Probe (WMAP) satellite results, is based on five years of accumulated observations. It is astronomers' most detailed all-sky map of the radiation from the cosmic creation event, also known as the cosmic background radiation. (Image courtesy of NASA/WMAP Science Team)

from that cosmic origin event have taught them more about its beginning, history, structure, and design than any other set of observations.

So far, the best maps of the radiation from the cosmic creation event come from the second and third data releases of the Wilkinson Microwave Anisotropy Probe (WMAP) satellite.[13] In analyzing these maps, astronomers have been able to calculate how much of the universe's original inventory of protons and neutrons were fused by the big bang into helium.[14] Such analysis even yields important information about the physical conditions of the universe just 10^{-34} seconds (a ten-billionth of a trillionth of a trillionth of a second) after its moment of beginning.

Theoretically, the earlier in cosmic history humans arrived, compared to 13.73 billion years, the smaller the fraction of cosmic history they could have observed. If humans had arrived significantly later upon the cosmic scene, the situation also would have been less than optimal. The accelerating expansion of the universe (due to the effect of dark energy) will eventually propel the cosmic origin event beyond the limits of viewing. At some point dark energy will expand the universe at speeds exceeding the velocity of light. Someday, the space surface along which light travels will be stretching that fast. (For an explanation of how that is possible, see "Exceeding the Light-Speed Limit," p. 56.) Dark energy implies that the later in cosmic history (after about 14 billion years from the beginning of the universe) humans arrive, the smaller the fraction of cosmic history they will be able to see.

Two physicists, Lawrence Krauss and Robert Scherrer, in a prize-winning essay on gravity, calculated that in the distant future, observers on any planet in the universe will be fundamentally unable to ascertain any of the universe's important features.[15] In particular, it will become impossible for any physical sentient being living anywhere within the cosmos to determine whether the universe is expanding or has a beginning. Researchers won't be able to learn anything about the origin of the elements or discover the existence of dark energy or map the temperature fluctuations in the cosmic background radiation. Cosmology as a science inevitably must come to an end.

Exceeding the Light-Speed Limit

Einstein's special theory of relativity establishes that no physical object can be accelerated from less than the velocity of light to beyond the velocity of light. This relativity rule, however, comes with two important caveats.

The first is that the special relativity rule holds for light traveling in a vacuum. The presence of a medium through which light travels affects the velocity of light to a small degree.

The second qualification is that the special relativity rule assumes that no dark energy is present. While dark energy has virtually no influence on objects located close to each other, it can expand the cosmic surface at *any* rate of velocity including velocities much greater than light's.

Everything in the universe—including all the planets, stars, galaxies, and matter and energy of the universe—is confined to its space-time surface. In an expanding universe, objects far apart from one another along the surface will continue to move away from one another (under the influence of cosmic expansion) at higher velocities than objects closer together.

When dark energy eventually expands the cosmic surface so rapidly that it pushes distant objects (relative to Earth) away at velocities greater than the velocity of light, then those objects will cease to be visible from Earth. Their light can never reach an observer's telescope. As dark energy continues to expand the cosmic surface at greater and greater velocities, more and more objects in the universe cease to be visible.

Powerful Purposes

Humans indeed are living at the only time in cosmic history when astronomers can see the entire history of the universe. This is our time not only to live but also to comprehend the miracle of our existence. Today scientists possess the tools to explore the origin and characteristics of the cosmos, to study its entire history. Their studies allow us to contemplate what lies beyond. Both science and philosophy are vitally involved in that discussion. More on this subject comes in the chapters ahead.

But first, a compelling question: Why would a loving God make only one planet capable of sustaining life? Perhaps he created other beings like us elsewhere in the cosmos. Chapter 4 sheds light on these oft-debated topics.

4

Why Such a Lonely Universe?

The human desire to reach out and touch someone seems irresistible. People travel to the ends of the Earth to make new friends and to enjoy adventures with those they love. (That's at least one reason passenger cars were invented.) Given ongoing advances in transportation and communications technology, it was inevitable that our desire to explore and search for intelligent life would extend beyond Earth to other parts of the Milky Way and to galaxies beyond.

And if any other beings exist in the universe, wouldn't they want to reach us, too? More than fifty years ago, this question became the subject of a now-famous conversation.

The Search for Answers

On a summer day in 1950, four distinguished physicists—Nobel laureate Enrico Fermi, father of the H-bomb Edward Teller, Emil Konopinski, and Herbert York—were on their way to lunch. As they walked toward Fuller Lodge at Los Alamos

This photograph of Fermi at the chalkboard was taken shortly before he framed his famous paradox about the existence of intelligent extraterrestrial life. (Image courtesy of Los Alamos National Laboratory/Photo Researchers, Inc.)

Figure 4.1. Enrico Fermi, Winner of the 1938 Nobel Prize in Physics

National Laboratory, New Mexico, the subject of flying saucers and extraterrestrials came up. Later Teller, Konopinski, and York recalled that over lunch Fermi laid out a paradox that went something like this:

Since the Milky Way Galaxy contains over a hundred billion stars, there could be as many as several billion planets orbiting around them. If civilizations similar to ours had developed on even a tiny fraction of those planets, and if just a fraction of those civilizations chose to explore and/or colonize other planets, traveling from one to another at a minute fraction of light's velocity, then the entire galaxy should have been explored or colonized within a few million years. Given that the Milky Way Galaxy is already several billion years old, Earth should have been visited and colonized long ago. So where is everybody?[1]

Fermi's point could be paraphrased as, "What's wrong with this picture?" He dared his associates to expose the error of his assumptions. That challenge led to a decades-long debate on the question "Are we alone?"

Have They Already Come?

While Fermi and his colleagues were considering the enigma he posed, speculation about UFOs (unidentified flying objects) was becoming a national craze. During the 1950s, the hysteria drove many Americans to conclude that extraterrestrial beings in exotic spacecraft were stealthily invading Earth for some mysterious, perhaps sinister, purpose. Today the notion that UFOs are physical spacecraft from interstellar space still prevails in popular opinion. Even some people in the highest echelons of government and academia say the answer to Fermi's question, "Where is everybody?" is that extraterrestrials have already come.

For the most part, the scientific community rejects that answer. After 60 years of investigation into several million UFO reports, researchers have concluded that 90 to 99 percent of all UFO sightings are, in fact, IFOs. Identifiable flying objects include natural phenomena, human-made (often experimental) aircraft, pranksters' hoaxes, and psychological phenomena. Of the remaining 1 to 10 percent, scientists have found no credible evidence (such as crash debris or physical artifacts) indicating that these sightings involve physical craft, with or without beings on board.

The publication of the Condon Report on Project Blue Book in 1969 did little, if anything, to quell public speculation about alien visitors, which continues unabated. However, subsequent rigorous interdisciplinary studies have yielded sufficient data to demonstrate that at least some of the residual (still unidentified 1–10 percent) UFOs are *real* and yet not tangible, or physical, in nature.[2] They may be categorized as occult or nonphysical manifestations.

Could They Come?

The four physicists who lunched together in Fuller Lodge knew that space travel at velocities greater than the speed of light is physically impossible. By 1950 overwhelming physical proof established that Einstein's theory of special relativity could not be violated at any time or anywhere in the universe.

However, scientists didn't know then that rocks, dust, gas, particles, and radiation so littered interstellar space that any spacecraft's travel speed would be severely limited. Damage to a spacecraft increases geometrically with collision velocity. If a rock hits a car's fender while the car is traveling 50 miles per hour, the collision energy would be 100 times greater than if the stone struck when the vehicle was moving 5 miles per hour. If that same rock struck the car traveling at just 1 percent of the velocity of light (about 6.7 million miles per hour) its collision energy would be 45 trillion times greater still. This geometric increase in collision damage with increasing collision velocity explains why, regardless of technological capability or financial resources, any hypothetical spaceship would need to limit its speed (to something less than 1 percent of light's velocity).

Such a damage hazard would also require that the trip be routed through relatively benign regions of interstellar space in heavily armored, radiation-shielded craft. Greater spacecraft travel speeds, longer trips, or more danger-ridden regions of interstellar space would result in extensive spacecraft destruction and the death of any onboard travelers.

Given the limitations imposed by the laws of physics and the conditions of interstellar space within the Milky Way Galaxy, a trip by physical intelligent aliens from another planetary system to Earth would take at least 25,000 years.[3] (To learn why, see "Are They Out There?" pp. 62–63.) That length of time implies multiple generations. As challenging as it might be to keep one generation focused on a single mission for their entire lives, the possibility of maintaining that focus throughout hundreds of generations seems hard to imagine.

A more fundamental problem for interstellar space travelers, however, is that a trip of more than 25,000 years exceeds any reasonable extinction time for the onboard inhabitants. It's one thing to keep a high-tech, intelligent species alive on a good-sized, resource-rich planet for that long (although even that possibility seems doubtful[4]); it's quite another to keep such a species alive, healthy, and goal-oriented for thousands of years within the confines of a spaceship.

For that matter, if human beings are any indication, it would be extraordinarily difficult to maintain sanity and peace among the craft's passengers for such an extended period of time (see "The Biosphere Experiment"). Nor would the limited environs of a spaceship be very tolerant of ecosystem disasters.

The Biosphere Experiment

Biosphere 2, located near Tucson, Arizona, allowed for simulation of conditions that would likely be encountered on a long-term space journey. For Mission 1, eight people lived in a $200 million, 3.15-acre artificially enclosed ecological capsule for a two-year period. During that time, carbon dioxide levels fluctuated wildly, nitrous oxide levels rose to toxic levels, oxygen plummeted, most of the vertebrate and all of the pollinating insects died, cockroaches multiplied out of control, and the human inhabitants suffered from malnutrition. Ultimately, oxygen had to be pumped in, nitrous oxide removed, and food delivered.

During Mission 2, seven people were to be enclosed for a ten-month period. Within the first few months, however, two members of the crew had to be replaced, and by the end of six months, the entire mission was aborted.

Scientists judged Biosphere 2 a failure because even basic ecological balances could not be sustained for more than a few months. Arguably a greater problem, though, was the experiment's effect on the crew members. Long periods of confinement in a limited space with just a few individuals produced psychological symptoms akin to what inmates experience in solitary confinement.

In one critical respect, Biosphere 2 could not be genuinely analogous to interstellar travel in a spaceship.[5] All of the biosphere inhabitants knew that if something went wrong, they could be rescued in a matter of minutes. They also had immediate verbal and visual contact with people outside the capsule. If they really needed something, it could be supplied. In a spaceship on its way to a distant planetary system, the response to a radio-communicated message would take several decades. If one or more crew members broke down under the pressure and started destroying the spaceship or harming other members of the mission, no outside help would be at hand. *Discover* magazine reported this comment by Russian cosmonaut Valery Ryumin: "All the conditions necessary for murder are met if you shut two men in a cabin and leave them together for two months."[6]

Civilizations capable of designing and launching spaceships would not likely ignore these complicating factors. Reasonable decision-makers would conclude that machines and robots have much better chances of surviving in interstellar space than do sentient beings. Psychological breakdowns would not be a risk for robots. The cost, though impossibly high for safe travel of living beings, might be more manageable for mechanical instruments. Then again, intelligent aliens might conclude that even mechanical instruments could not survive interstellar trips sufficiently intact and/or that the cost would be impossibly high.

Are They Out There?

Years ago, an astronomy professor friend of mine asked his students on an exam, "What is the hottest spot (known) in the Milky Way Galaxy at the three-meter wavelength?" The answer at that time: Mount Wilson.

This 5,710-foot-high peak overlooking the Los Angeles Basin boasts the highest density of radio and television broadcasting antennae of any location in the world. At certain wavelengths, its radiation brightness temperature exceeds 100 billion degrees. Such an extremely high temperature implies that if intelligent creatures with advanced technology were living in some nearby planetary system, they would be well aware of our existence.

Given that earthlings broadcast their presence (intentionally or otherwise) throughout local interstellar space, several astronomers concluded that if intelligent life exists elsewhere in this galaxy and has the goal of making contact with another civilization, then it would *not* be difficult to detect their signals. This realization gave birth to the SETI Institute, dedicated to the search for extraterrestrial intelligence.

The SETI Institute has been ongoing for nearly fifty years. Project Phoenix ranks as its deepest search conducted to date. That project scanned every star within 200 light-years of Earth that either manifests solarlike characteristics or is known to possess planets, listening for intelligible signals. None with the power output of airport radar beams (or greater) have been detected anywhere within the vicinity of these 800 stars.[7]

For the past several years, astronomers have aggressively searched for planets beyond our solar system. While the search tools aren't yet sensitive enough to detect planets like Earth, they can easily detect planets the size of Jupiter and Saturn. That's helpful because without such planets in their vicinity, advanced life on any habitable planets cannot be sustained.

Jupiter and Saturn operate as gravitational shields for Earth. They protect it from catastrophic hits by asteroids and comets that would render advanced civilization impossible.[8] If either Jupiter or Saturn were any less massive or any more distant, such protection would be inadequate.

So far, astronomers have discovered more than 280 extrasolar planets orbiting more than 230 stars.[9] Of these extrasolar planets, 256 are the mass of Saturn or greater. However, among them, none has the characteristics that would permit the existence of a neighboring planet (in the same planetary system) capable of supporting advanced life and advanced civilization.

For the past forty years, astronomers have looked far and wide within the Milky Way Galaxy for a solar twin—a star with all the essential-for-advanced-life characteristics of our star, the Sun. Such a star might conceivably be orbited by a planet capable of supporting intelligent life. The three astronomers most active in searching for a solar twin have reported that despite decades of intense observational effort, "no perfect solar twin has been found to date."[10]

All these null results strongly suggest that at least in our region of the Milky Way Galaxy, we humans are alone. This outcome has done little to dampen the enthusiasm of the SETI community, however. They argue that our local galactic region must be anomalous in some way. They claim that if we broaden our search to more distant parts of the galaxy, we *will* find other intelligent life. The Copernican Principle (described on p. 65), in part, gives impetus to this line of reasoning.

A Matter of Mediocrity

Early Greek astronomers used careful measurements and plane geometry to determine the diameter of both the Earth and the

Moon and the approximate distance to the Sun, as well as to establish that the Sun is much larger than Earth, that stars are extremely distant, and that all the visible planets revolve around the Sun.[11] Without technology and additional mathematical tools (such as algebra) to support their Sun-centered perspective, however, their findings eventually fell victim to sociocultural forces: human ego and a serious theological fallacy.

Faulty logic and interpretation dictated that if humanity is the pinnacle of creation—the reason for the universe's existence—then humanity must reside at the physical center of the universe. All astronomical bodies should revolve around humanity's home, planet Earth. So geocentrism replaced the Greeks' heliocentrism as the prevailing view of the universe. And when simple mathematical tools initially predicted the positions of the planets in this Earth-centered view, it received apparent objective verification. As Western ideas spread, this notion became more firmly entrenched.

Such thinking persisted until the sixteenth century, when a Polish astronomer named Copernicus visited the great Italian libraries. Rediscovering and comprehending the earlier Greek proofs that the Earth and all the known planets revolve around the Sun, Copernicus helped resurrect heliocentrism. Despite heated debate, the idea of a Sun-centered universe stuck, primarily because by this time Europeans possessed sufficiently advanced mathematical tools.

As curiosity and technology yielded increasingly better telescopes, astronomers discovered that Earth's star—the Sun—and its planets are part of a much bigger and more geometrically complex universe. They discovered that Earth does not reside at the center of the solar system, nor does the solar system reside anywhere near the center of the Milky Way Galaxy.

Eventually scientists determined that the Milky Way Galaxy is not the dominant galaxy in the Local Group, nor is it at the center of the Local Group. They found that the Local Group is one of the smallest galaxy clusters in the Virgo supercluster and that it resides on the far edge of that supercluster. The Virgo supercluster, in turn, proves to be far from the center of a cluster of superclusters of galaxies.

Astronomers established that the universe has *no* physical center (see chapter 2). Everything physical about the universe—all of its stars, galaxies, energy, and matter—resides on its surface in much the same way as life and civilization reside on Earth's surface.

Earth's galaxy cluster, galaxy, solar system, and planet—not to mention the human population—began to seem small and insignificant. Evolutionary theory fueled belief that humanity is merely one step in a progression of more or less random natural processes.

This seeming insignificance compelled several late twentieth-century cosmologists to introduce the Copernican Principle, the idea that Earth holds neither a central nor a favored position in the universe. In its farthest extension, the Copernican Principle assigns the same nondescript status to human beings. It claims that humanity occupies no special or privileged place in the cosmos. However, more recent scientific discoveries show problems with both the basic and extended versions of the principle. These new discoveries carry important implications for humanity.

It's a Jungle Out There

Not all locales within our galaxy would make desirable homesteads for advanced life. For example, anywhere near the center of the Milky Way Galaxy (as of any galaxy), lethal radiation emanates from a massive black hole, as well as from a jam of supernova remnants and gigantic stars. Also, given the density of stars and molecular clouds there, the gravity from such objects would certainly disturb the orbits of any possible planets far more radically than life can tolerate.

These deadly conditions extend outward more than 20,000 light-years from the galactic core. Earth's solar system orbits at a distance of 26,000 light-years.[12] Even at this distance, radiation remains a factor—unless the solar system stays protected within the plane of the spinning galaxy's disk. Virtually all stars bounce up and down, above and below the galactic plane. As soon as they do, any planets orbiting them get blasted with radiation from the galactic core. Within the plane, however, thick dust provides a radiation shield. Because our solar system experiences very little up and down movement in its orbit about the galactic center,[13] Earth's life remains protected behind that radiation shield.

Planetary systems farther out than 26,000 light-years from the galaxy's core face a different problem. Heavy elements (needed for advanced life's existence and survival) are sparse at such distances. Only within a narrow ring (annulus) about 26,000 light-years distant from the galactic core does advanced life stand a chance. Astronomers call this region the galactic habitable zone.[14]

Ironically, most areas within the galactic habitable zone aren't all that livable. The galaxy's spiral arms plus giant stars, star clusters, dense molecular clouds, and young supernova remnants intersect large segments of the so-called habitable region. All these bodies either emit deadly radiation, unleash severe dust storms, and/or cause gravitational disturbances. Earth's solar system, at least for now, resides far from any of these perils (see figure 4.2, p. 67).

Even a planetary system in a rare safe zone won't likely stay safe for long. The spiral structure of a galaxy like the Milky Way rotates at a certain rate while stars (and their planets) within the galaxy revolve around the center at different rates, depending on their distance from the galactic core.

Stars close to the center take a few million years to complete one orbit while stars much farther from the center take a billion years or more. The spiral structure itself takes about a quarter of a billion years to make one rotation. These rate differences mean that most stars will pass through—or find themselves overtaken by—the spiral arms at relatively frequent intervals.

Picture a racetrack. The main cluster of cars is being lapped by the fastest cars. That main pack laps the slower cars. Each time these faster or slower cars encounter the larger group, the space between vehicles tightens, increasing the danger of collisions. When fast-moving stars pass through the spiral arms or the arms move past slow-moving stars, the planets orbiting those stars are exposed to the arms' deadly conditions.

The solar system holds a special position in the Milky Way, close to (but not exactly at) the co-rotation distance—the one distance from the core where stars orbit the galaxy at the same rate as its

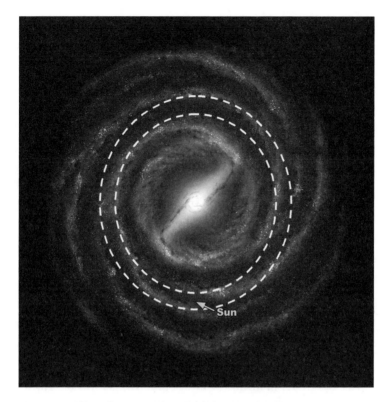

Figure 4.2. The Safe Spot within the Galactic Habitable Zone

This artist's rendering offers a detailed reconstruction of the structure of the Milky Way Galaxy (minus the 150 globular clusters). The solar system's location is within a narrow annulus (between the dotted circles), where protection from the dangers of the galactic core is possible. The quantity and variety of heavy elements and long-lived radiometric isotopes that advanced life requires are also available. Earth's solar system currently resides at a spot along the annulus far from any risks to advanced life such as spiral arms, young supernova remnants, dense molecular clouds, and super-giant stars. (Image courtesy of NASA/JPL-Caltech/R. Hurt [SSC])

spiral arm structure does. A star or planetary system located at the co-rotation distance and between two spiral arms would seemingly remain in that safe place. However, stars and planetary systems *exactly at* the co-rotation distance would experience a "mean motion resonance," repeated gravitational "kicks" exerted by the galactic arm structure. Such kicks would send the star and its possible planetary system flying out of the habitable zone.

A Prime Location

Earth's solar system is located just inside the co-rotation distance. So it is safe from the mean motion resonance. Because the solar system revolves around the galactic center only slightly faster than the galactic arm structure, it crosses the spiral arms only once about every billion years. The last spiral arm crossing occurred 560 to 600 million years ago (just before the Cambrian explosion, when complex animals first came on the scene), so Earth currently resides in the safest possible position.

This protected location is truly exceptional. Not all spiral galaxies are like the Milky Way. In the vast majority, the co-rotation distance and the habitable zone fail to overlap. Not only is there a match for the Milky Way Galaxy, but also the best possible place for a newly forming planetary system to accumulate all the heavy elements and long-lived radioactive isotopes required for advanced life happens to lie just inside the co-rotation distance.

The Milky Way Galaxy is extraordinary in two other respects. First, as figure 4.2 illustrates (see p. 67), the Milky Way Galaxy's spiral arms are exceptionally symmetrical and evenly spaced with respect to one another. Second, the arms are approximately the same size.

What's more, the Milky Way's spiral arms show no signs of the disturbing events found in most other spiral galaxies, such as giant and highly active star-forming regions, large and active supernova remnants, enormous molecular clouds, warped and/or disturbed arm features, and a multiplicity of spurs and feathers between the arms. Unlike other spiral galaxies, including its immediate neighbor, the Andromeda Galaxy[15] (see figure 1.1, p. 21), the Milky Way Galaxy has experienced no significant collision or merger events with other galaxies over the past 10 billion years.[16] When we compare the characteristics of other spiral galaxies that come close to matching those of the Milky Way, its unique features for life support become all the more apparent (see figure 4.3).

Another distinctive of the Milky Way Galaxy is the galaxy cluster in which it resides. Nearly all other galaxies in the universe reside within dense clusters of galaxies, with giant or supergiant galaxies as neighbors (see figure 4.4). These giants and supergiants

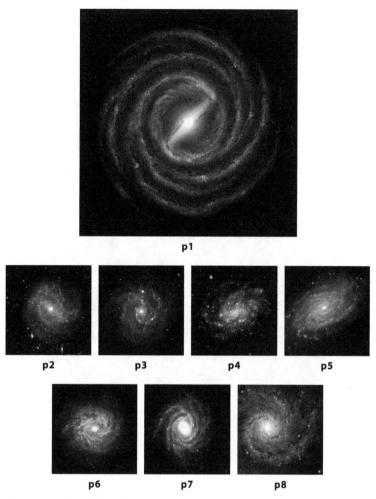

Figure 4.3. The Milky Way Galaxy Compared to Other Spiral Galaxies

The Milky Way Galaxy shows amazing symmetry in its spiral arm structure. It also displays little evidence of any recent internal and external major disturbance events. These features set the Milky Way apart in its capacity to support advanced life. (Panel 1: Image courtesy of R. Hurt [SSC]/ JPL-Caltech/NASA; Panel 2: Image courtesy of William Keel/University of Alabama; Panel 3: Image courtesy of Al Kelly [JSCAS/NASA] & Arne Henden [Flagstaff/USNO]; Panel 4: Image courtesy of NASA/JPL-Caltech/OCIW; Panel 5: Image courtesy of NASA/ESA, The Hubble Heritage Team and A. Riess [STScI]; Panel 6: Image courtesy of European Space Agency and Stephen Smartt [University of Cambridge]; Panel 7: Image courtesy of European Southern Observatory; Panel 8: Image courtesy of NASA, ESA, and the Hubble Heritage [STScI/AURA]-ESA/Hubble Collaboration)

Figure 4.4. The Coma Cluster of Galaxies

A typical cluster of galaxies, the Coma Cluster contains a few supergiant elliptical galaxies, hundreds of medium- and large-sized elliptical galaxies, a few spiral galaxies, and thousands of dwarf galaxies. The Coma Cluster is 370 million light-years away. This image shows its central region. Virtually every spot or smudge of light is a galaxy. (Image courtesy of Jean-Charles Cuillandre/ Canada-France-Hawaii Telescope/Photo Researchers, Inc.)

intermittently blast their whole neighborhood with deadly radiation. Also, their gravity and the gravity of the thousands of smaller galaxies associated with them significantly distort the structures of the galaxies they contain. Thus, advanced life is not possible for galaxies dwelling in typical galaxy clusters.

The Milky Way Galaxy finds itself in a tiny cluster of galaxies without any giants or supergiants nearby and where the galaxies are widely dispersed. A typical galaxy cluster contains more than 10,000 closely packed galaxies. The Milky Way's cluster, called "the Local

Group," contains only about forty galaxies—two medium-sized (Andromeda and the Milky Way) and the rest small or dwarf.

Here the Goldilocks principle of being "just right" becomes even more obvious. The Local Group (see figure 4.5) is spread apart in such a way that the Milky Way's spiral structure remains largely undisturbed—an important requirement for the possibility of harboring advanced life. At the same time, the Local Group contains a sufficient number of the smaller dwarf galaxies to sustain the spiral structure of the Milky Way. (Star formation drives the spiral arm structure, and the infusion of gas and dust from dwarf galaxies keeps the star formation rate high enough.) Unless Earth's galaxy absorbs a smallish dwarf galaxy about once every half-billion to one billion years, its spiral structure will inevitably collapse.

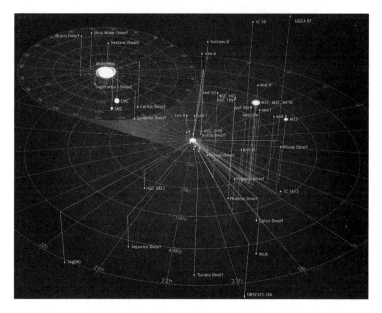

Figure 4.5. The Local Group of Galaxies

The top figure shows a three-dimensional map of all the galaxies in the Local Group except those in the immediate vicinity of the Milky Way Galaxy. The bottom figure shows a magnified (10X) view of the Milky Way and its entourage of dwarf and subdwarf galaxies. Unlike typical clusters of galaxies, the Local Group contains only a few dozen galaxies, all of which are well spread apart and none of which are medium-sized or larger elliptical galaxies. (Image courtesy of Mark Garlick/ Science Photo Library)

Not only do galaxies reside in clusters, the clusters themselves exist in clusters of clusters called superclusters. Here again, Earth's location favors life's needs. The Local Group sits on the extreme outer fringe of the Virgo supercluster. If it were closer to the middle, Virgo's mostly massive clusters would disrupt the Local Group or swallow it up. Either way, its suitability for life would be destroyed.

Astronomers' discoveries about the rarity of life-habitable locations in the universe challenge Enrico Fermi's proposition that the cosmos could be filled with inhabitants. While Earth's location is not geographically central to the solar system, galaxy, galaxy cluster, or galaxy supercluster, it deserves the description "spectacularly favored" for life. Perhaps Someone had a purpose or purposes in mind for limiting life to just one residence.

Real estate brokers often say the key to property value is location, location, location. If this principle applies to the cosmic scene, Earth's location would be considered way beyond "prime." No amount of money could buy it. Earth appears to reside in the only neighborhood in the universe where humans can exist and thrive long enough to enjoy a global, high-tech civilization and to discover how rare they are.

Various SETI projects have scoured our neighborhood only to find vacancy signs. It certainly appears that humans are the only species advanced enough to attempt an answer to Fermi's question, "Are we alone?"

But what about other life-forms? Is the universe devoid of any and all other kinds of physical life? Isn't it possible that life could have spontaneously generated from nonlife in a wide range of environments? And if so, wouldn't it naturally progress from molecules to something much more complex, perhaps something as extremely complex as humans? Biochemists' and physicists' discoveries provide some invaluable data for answering these questions.

Finding Simple Life

During the graduate course I took from Carl Sagan, during which he speculated about intelligent life in the universe (see chapter 1, pp. 22–23), he also outlined the naturalistic model for the origin of life. Sagan spoke about a vast primordial soup richly endowed with prebiotic molecules that percolated and slowly evolved through "billions of years" into a very simple life-form from which all future life naturally evolved. He reiterated this explanation in several of his writings.[17]

Nearly forty years later, the story line has changed dramatically. Origin-of-life researchers now recognize that at most only a few million years transpired between the first possible opportunity for life to exist on Earth and the appearance of the first life-forms.[18]

The twentieth century's widely accepted scenario for life's origin has been challenged also because the geological record reveals no evidence of Earth's supposed primordial soup, whether in oceans or ponds or on mineral substrates. The carbon signature in Earth's most ancient rocks contradicts the traditional explanation.

Dead organisms leave behind (in ancient strata) carbonaceous residues with a distinct ratio of carbon-13 compared to carbon-12 and of nitrogen-15 compared to nitrogen-14, a ratio that differs noticeably from the buildup of carbonaceous substances that arose chemically from inorganic compounds. Measurements of carbon and nitrogen isotope ratios in multiple ancient deposits show that none of the carbonaceous material in those deposits formed from prebiotic material.[19] These findings imply that the quantity of prebiotics on and in ancient Earth amounted to zero.

Physicists have discovered at least one fundamental reason for the lack of prebiotics—the oxygen-ultraviolet paradox. If oxygen is present in the terrestrial environment, even in tiny amounts, it inhibits the production of prebiotics. However, without oxygen's presence, the Sun's ultraviolet radiation penetrates the environment, causing the destruction of prebiotic compounds. Both oxygen and ultraviolet radiation frustrate prebiotic chemistry. Thus, with or without oxygen in Earth's environment, prebiotic chemistry would have failed to produce biologically significant molecules.

Without prebiotics, no reasonable possibility remains for a naturalistic origin of life on Earth. This conclusion, more than any other, led to the launch of science's newest disciplines—astrobiology and astrobiochemistry. Astrobiology is the search for life in outer space and the study of how that life, if it exists, might have been transported to Earth. In spite of much funding and searching, astrobiologists have failed to find any trace of evidence for extraterrestrial life.

Pursuing a less lofty goal, astrobiochemists search for the chemical building blocks of life in outer space and the pathways by which such building blocks might be brought to Earth. Over 120 organic type molecules, including 3-carbon sugars, have been discovered in the interstellar medium and in comets.[20] However, astrobiochemists have yet to find any of the simplest building blocks for life—no amino acids (the chemical building blocks for proteins), no nucleobases, and none of the 5- and 6-carbon sugars critical for linking together the nucleobases (the chemical building blocks for DNA and RNA).

Recent claims for the discovery of low levels of glycine (the simplest of the amino acids) and for pyrimidine (a nucleobase) in interstellar molecular clouds have been withdrawn.[21] While the possibility remains that such simple building-block molecules may yet be discovered, the upper limits already established on their abundances are so extremely low as to render them useless for any naturalistic origin-of-life scenario.

Such restrictions are consistent with the known physical and chemical conditions of outer space. These conditions, especially the ever-present ultraviolet and X-ray radiation, guarantee that as quickly or slowly as the building-block molecules might be constructed, they will be destroyed. As for the very low levels of a few of the biologically significant amino acids found in a small percentage of meteorites, researchers concede that much and possibly all of what they have found may actually represent terrestrial contamination by Earth's life or the remains of Earth's life.[22]

An additional barricade, the homochirality problem, virtually vaporizes any hope that even the simplest extraterrestrial life could have arisen by naturalistic means. Homochirality refers to the fact that of the twenty amino acids that assemble to form proteins, nineteen must be "left-handed" rather than "right-handed" in their configuration. (The other amino acid has only one configuration.) And, in the assembly of replicator molecules (DNA and RNA), only right-handed sugars can be used.

One problem for naturalistic origin-of-life scenarios is the lack of any realistic mechanism either on Earth or anywhere else in the universe for generating reservoirs of these building-block molecules that manifest only left-handed or right-handed configurations.[23] A second problem is that all environments outside of living organisms will quickly drive any single-handed or homochiral reservoir into a random mixture of left- and right-handed molecules.

One Viable Option

More than fifty years have passed since the flask experiments by Stanley Miller and Harold Urey rekindled the primordial soup hypothesis for the origin of life. Scientists now realize, however, that generating miniscule amounts of a few amino acids is irrelevant to the origin of life because the chemicals in Miller and Urey's experiment were exposed to neither oxygen nor ultraviolet light. The fact that Earth never possessed measurable quantities of prebiotics (see p. 73) and that the universe appears devoid of reservoirs for life's fundamental chemical building blocks (see p. 74) also argues for the famed experiment's irrelevance.

As far back as 1973, a deep sense of frustration over any possible naturalistic explanation for life's origin on Earth or anywhere else within the vast reaches of interstellar space led Francis Crick (who shared the Nobel Prize for the discovery of the double helix nature of DNA) and Leslie Orgel (one of the world's preeminent origin-of-life researchers) to suggest that intelligent aliens must have salted Earth with bacteria about 3.8 billion years ago.[24] This suggestion, however intriguing or bizarre, fails to answer the question of where the aliens might have come from. It also contradicts evidence that shows intelligent life could not have arrived on the cosmic scene any sooner than about 13.7 billion years after the cosmic origin event. The implausibility of interstellar space travel also remains an intractable problem.

Ruling out a visit by aliens from a planetary system far, far away narrows the reasonable options down to one: Something or Someone from beyond the physics and dimensions of the universe, who is not subject to them, placed life and humanity in the only location in the universe at the only time in cosmic history where and when such creatures could survive and thrive.

Alone in the Cosmos

Current understanding of the universe, at least from a naturalistic perspective, supports the idea that only Earth offers a sufficiently hospitable environment for an intelligent species to survive and build a high-tech civilization. It also confirms that Earth may offer the only hospitable environment for the simplest of life-forms. Since advanced life can exist only if supported by billions of years of previously existing simpler life, it seems doubly certain that the humanity of Earth is the only intelligent physical species in the observable universe.

After nearly sixty years of researching answers to Fermi's paradox, science's reply to his question, "Where is everybody?" boils down to "Nowhere but here." However, this conclusion does not mean humankind must be alone in an absolute sense as some nontheists propose.

Not So Alone

Physicist Victor Stenger, in his book *God: The Failed Hypothesis*, approaches much of the data cited above from a different and some might even say a cynical perspective. While theists view the contrast between the exceptional conditions of Earth for the support of human beings and civilization and the extremely hostile nature of the rest of the universe as evidence for supernatural intention and design, Stenger sees the inhospitableness of the cosmos as an indication that life and humanity cannot be "high on the universe's agenda."[25]

In addition to noting the geographical hostility of the universe, Stenger comments on its temporal hostility. He points out that such inevitable events as the coming incineration of Earth by the Sun (when it enters the red giant phase) and the eventual burning out of all stars unequivocally limits humanity's cosmic longevity.

Stenger sees the hostility of the universe as proof of God's non-existence. He writes, "Even taking the most optimistic view of the future of humankind . . . , it is hard to conclude that the universe was created with a special, cosmic purpose for humanity."[26] To him it seems "inconceivable that a creator exists who has a special love for humanity, and then just relegated it to a tiny point in space and time."[27] He argues that humanity not only is alone in the cosmos but is imprisoned inside a tiny bubble within the vastness of the universe.[28] For Stenger, this solitary confinement of humanity eliminates any possibility of a loving Creator—certainly of a God who cares for humanity.

The theist, and particularly the Christian theist, says that even if we humans are the only sentient physical species in the cosmos, we are not necessarily and absolutely alone. We are not the only life. There is a Life from which our life comes. According to a Christian worldview, humans were created, deliberately, in the image of God.[29] Any human at any time can communicate with the Source of all life—the One who created matter, energy, space, time, and individual persons. Anyone can receive his help, comfort, guidance, wisdom, and capacity to care for others. Also, through prayer, any human at any time and place can play a part in the life of any other person. Thus, from a Christian perspective, people can be connected to God and to one another in meaningful and fulfilling relationships.

It seems understandable that nontheists would judge the universe a lonely, unloving, even pointless place *if* the universe were, as Carl Sagan described it, "all that is or ever was or ever will be."[30] And yet even those who reject God's existence and purposes for humanity seem to experience some measure of delight and wonder as they participate in exploring and colonizing the entirety of our planet. Despite our twenty-first-century knowledge and technological advance, we humans still have much more to learn about Earth and its creatures just to fulfill the basic planet-care commands God gave the first human beings.[31]

Furthermore, the Christian worldview says humans are not the only species of intelligent life in the universe. In addition to creating animals and people, God created angels. Though angels are not subject to the limitations of the laws of physics and the dimensions of length, width, height, and time, they are nonetheless able to enter the human realm. The Bible describes many instances of humans' relating to angels.[32] The book of Hebrews says "some people have entertained angels without knowing it" (13:2).

More importantly, God has never left humanity without a witness to his presence and personal care for us. For centuries he spoke through prophets, then in person as Jesus of Nazareth. When Jesus physically left planet Earth, he sent the Holy Spirit to be with his followers, promising never to leave them, never to forsake them—even to "the very end" (see Matt. 28:18–20).

The nontheist who recognizes that human survivability on Earth has limits sees only nothingness beyond. Those who accept that limitation *and* the Bible's message about what lies beyond recognize the universe as preparation for something more. God is using time, space, matter, energy, and all the features of the cosmos to prepare people—all who are willing—to receive an inheritance of love, joy, beauty, truth, and connectedness surpassing what anyone can possibly imagine (see 1 Cor. 2:9).

Consider the way parents prepare their children to explore and relate to the world and the rest of humanity. Step-by-step, as the little one matures, father and mother allow the world of exploration and relationships to expand. Likewise, according to the Bible, God will allow his children to move beyond their smallish playground (planet Earth) into the expansive realm (the new creation) he always intended for them to experience and enjoy. However, just as parents with their young, God waits to open the door from Earth to the new creation until we are prepared to receive and enjoy all it has to offer.

Why the preparation for our eventual entry into the new creation demands certain temporary restrictions and "lonely" aspects in our relationship capabilities is addressed in chapter 6 and in chapters 8 through 12. The expansiveness of this new habitat and the nature of relationships there are described in chapter 13, which offers a short preview of our life in the new creation. But first, a few more questions need a response: Why is the universe such a dark place, and why is Earth situated in one of the darkest corners of the cosmos? Chapter 5 addresses both.

5

Why Such a Dark Universe?

In sunny Southern California, almost every car on the road has tinted windows. For Beth, Hannah, Scott, and other RTB staff who live west of the office, dark sunglasses are a must. Driving home just before sunset on the 10 or 210 freeways, they can face a blinding glare.

Typically we think of light as helpful to visibility, but in some cases it's the opposite. The car's dome light after dark causes problems for the driver. And no one wants the lights left on during a movie or slide show. For an astronomer, light can be an enemy.

Researchers who believe in a personal Creator (and many do) thank their Maker for Earth's placement in one of the darkest regions of the universe. Not only are the quantities and locations of the various kinds of dark stuff exactly what advanced life needs, but because of Earth's dark cosmic location, the lights of the universe don't blind us or limit our view. Astronomers can see virtually all of the heavens' wonders, including the entirety of cosmic history.[1]

This visibility is possible because Earth resides in a very dark place. In fact, Earth's solar system resides in the darkest part of the Milky Way Galaxy's life-habitable zone. And the Milky Way resides in the darkest life-habitable region of its galaxy cluster, which occupies the darkest life-habitable region of its supercluster of galaxies.

Dark Moon

Astronomers tend to complain about moonlight. Its glow sometimes limits their attempts to make quality observations of distant, faint objects in the universe. At major optical observatories, telescope time for research on galaxies and quasars must be limited to just a few days around a new Moon or to those few hours during the night when the Moon is below the horizon. For the remainder of the 29-day lunar cycle, more than half the available telescope time must be limited to objects so bright (typically stars in our galaxy) that the Moon's light does not radically disturb the quality of astronomical observation.

Scientists who specialize, as I did, in observing quasars and galaxies often lament that their research would be easier if the Moon were much smaller or if no Moon existed at all to illuminate the sky. But that's only hyperbole. Every astronomer realizes the Moon must be as big as it is for humans to exist, let alone for the possibility of research.

The Moon's large mass relative to Earth's, the Moon's proximity to Earth, and the fact that the Moon is solo all play a crucial role in stabilizing the tilt of Earth's rotation axis.[2] Other planets in our solar system which have either no moons or moons of relatively insignificant mass (compared to their planet's mass) experience chaotic tilting of their rotation axis.[3] The stability of Earth's rotation axis, tilted at 23.5 degrees, over a long period of time protects Earth's life from disastrous climate changes.

Calculations done by British astronomer Dave Waltham demonstrate, however, that Earth's rotation axis tilt would still be stable if the Moon were only half as massive as it is.[4] A less massive Moon would be smaller in the night sky and thus less disturbing to astronomers' attempts to study distant galaxies and quasars. Waltham also demonstrated, though, that unless the Moon is as massive as it is, its gravity would be insufficient to have slowed Earth's rotation rate to the twenty-four hours per day that human life and civilization require.[5] If days were longer than twenty-four hours, day-to-night temperature extremes would be too great. Yet with shorter days rainfall and benign temperatures would not be so evenly distributed over all the continental landmasses.

Another reason Earth needs the Moon's precise mass and present proximity has to do with their influence on tides. A Moon less massive or more distant from Earth and, therefore, smaller in the nighttime sky would mean weaker tides. Tides as powerful as those on Earth are necessary to effectively cleanse the coastal seawaters from toxins and to enrich them with nutrients. In fact, the Moon's specific properties are fine-tuned for life in so many different ways that one astronomer wrote an entire book on the subject in 1993.[6]

The recognition that the Moon must be as large as it is for people to exist definitely tempers any complaints astronomers make about light "pollution." These gripes are further tempered by the recognition that the Moon has an extraordinarily dark surface. It reflects a mere 7 percent of its incident light. Earth, by comparison, reflects 39 percent, some of Jupiter's and Saturn's moons reflect 60 to 90 percent, and Neptune reflects 73 percent.[7] Because the Moon is so exceptionally dark, or non-reflective (see figure 5.1), its bounced-back light presents a minor annoyance to astronomers rather than a blinding glow that obliterates astronomers' work and everyone else's enjoyment of the night sky.

Dark Planetary Companions

Other than the Sun and Moon, the brightest objects in Earth's sky are planets. But an amazing arrangement within the solar system prevents their luminosities from posing any significant hindrance to astronomers' capacity to study the universe.

Venus and Mars are the nearest planets to Earth. Mars is small and reflects just 15 percent of its incident light. Its orbital path puts Mars close to Earth only once every 26 months. Venus is an inner planet. Its reflective surface is 3.21 times larger than Mars' and has a reflectivity of 65 percent. However, because it orbits between Earth and the Sun, Venus affects only twilight viewing

Figure 5.1. The Dark Lunar Surface

Astronauts Edgar D. Mitchell (foreground) and Alan B. Shepard (background) set up the Active Seismic Experiment during the Apollo 14 mission to the Moon. The dark, low-reflectivity nature of the lunar surface is evident when contrasted with the light reflecting off the astronauts' spacesuits. Because of the Moon's dark, low-reflectivity surface, astronomers on Earth are able to make observations of night sky objects even when the Moon is up. (Image courtesy of NASA Kennedy Space Center [NASA-KSC])

of the night sky. Even then, only a thin crescent of its illuminated side faces Earth during the near-Earth part of its orbit.

If Venus and Mars traded places, Venus would be about ten times brighter at its closest approach to Earth than it is now, and it would remain bright all night long. Attempts to investigate the heavens anywhere near the position of Venus would be seriously problematic. If Mars and Jupiter traded places, the situation would be far worse. Jupiter, when closest to Earth, would become 1,550 times brighter in the night sky, about the same brightness as the quarter-phase Moon (half the illumination of a full Moon). Again, observation of galaxies would be impossible in such light conditions.

The gas giant planets in our solar system reside far from the Sun and far from us. Their distances limit both the amount of sunlight they reflect and how much of that reflected light reaches Earth. So none of the solar system's large planets place any significant limit on researchers' capacity to study the universe. Clearly, the positions and characteristics of the planets are fine-tuned to provide observers on Earth with a dark enough night sky that they can measure virtually all the features of the universe and record all its history.

The question here arises, why bother with this phenomenal planetary design if the intent is solely to ensure that astronomers on Earth can do research? Why not simply dispense with the other solar system planets altogether? The answer lies in the planets' rarely recognized role.

Like the Moon, Earth's planetary companions provide critical protection for life here. The gas giant planets—Jupiter, Saturn, Uranus, and Neptune—work together to shield Earth from life-exterminating collision events. Each gas giant acts like a gravitational blocker either to absorb or to deflect potential colliders such as asteroids and comets.

If the gas giant planets were any smaller, more distant, or less numerous, Earth would be pelted more frequently and more disastrously for life. On the other hand, if the gravitational pull of the gas giant planets were too great (as a result of their being closer or more massive), or if the gas giants' relative positions produced certain gravitational resonances, the result would be a disturbance to the life-critical orbit of Earth. Remarkably, Mars, Venus, and Mercury are exquisitely positioned to break up such resonances. Thus, the solar system's planets are fine-tuned in two ways: (1) they maximize the observational capabilities of Earth's inhabitants, and (2) they provide essential protection for all life.

Distant Star Clusters

Like all galaxies, the Milky Way is filled with bright beacons of light. If Earth were close to any of them, astronomical research would be seriously crippled.

The brightest lights in the Milky Way Galaxy are its core and its spiral arms (see figure 4.2). Located far from the galactic core, our solar system maintains an orbit about the center of the galaxy that keeps it within the galactic plane. Here, a thin disk of dust protects the solar system from the deadly X-ray and gamma-ray radiation that emanates from the galactic core. That same dust layer also blocks out most of the blazingly bright light shining from the thousands of dense star clusters situated in the core that otherwise would ruin astronomers' efforts to explore the universe.

In its orbit about the galactic center, the solar system rides almost exactly halfway between two spiral arms, the Perseus Arm and the Sagittarius Arm. Because of the solar system's position, the arms' crowded clusters of bright stars do not overly illuminate Earth's night sky. Nor do the thick dust clouds that reside in many parts of the arms block significant regions of the cosmos from our view. In short, thanks to the solar system's exceptional placement within the Milky Way Galaxy, these bright star clusters and dust clouds do not seriously thwart astronomers' efforts to learn about the origin, structure, and history of the galaxy and of the universe as a whole. See figure 4.2 for a precise, data-based reconstruction of the Milky Way.

One major source of potential light interference could not be included in figure 4.2 because it would have obscured astronomers' depiction of the spiral arm structure (the main point of the figure). That additional source: the Milky Way's array of intensely bright globular clusters. The Milky Way contains more than 150 such star clusters. Each packs from 10,000 to 10,000,000 stars into a region ranging from 10 to 200 light-years across. (Figure 5.2 on p. 85 provides an example.) If even one of these clusters were in the solar system's vicinity, the night sky would be bathed with intense light. Furthermore, because these clusters are stationary with respect to the background stars and galaxies (unlike the Moon and planets), they would permanently impair our view of those stars and galaxies within the regions they cover.

The nearest globular cluster, a relatively dim one as globular clusters go, is more than 7,000 light-years away, and the brightest is more than 15,000 light-years away. Their distant placement also contributes to Earth's ideal conditions for making astronomical observations.

Figure 5.2. The Globular Cluster Omega Centauri

This globular cluster contains an estimated 10 million stars. It is about 16,000 light-years away. If the globular cluster Omega Centauri were located anywhere near our solar system, its size and light would seriously limit astronomers' observations of the Milky Way Galaxy and the universe. (Image courtesy of NOAO/Science Photo Library)

Dark Nebulae

Astronomers can also be thankful the Milky Way Galaxy contains no bright star-forming gas clouds or gaseous nebulae. Virtually all spiral galaxies feature some gigantic ones, such as the Tarantula Nebula located in a dwarf galaxy known as the Large Magellanic Cloud (see figure 5.3 on p. 86), but the Milky Way does not. While it certainly does contain a number of gaseous nebulae, it contains no giants. And the gaseous nebulae in Earth's galactic home, unlike those in other spiral galaxies, are evenly distributed throughout its spiral arms.

What's more, no gaseous nebulae reside in the vicinity of the solar system. The nearest and brightest star-forming region is the

Figure 5.3. The Tarantula Nebula

The Tarantula Nebula (a gaseous nebula or star-forming gas cloud) is about 170,000 light-years away. If it were as close to Earth as the nearest stellar nursery, the Orion Nebula, it would block out over 40° or 80 full Moon diameters of the night sky. It would be 10 times brighter than Venus at its brightest and would cast shadows. (Image courtesy of NASA and the Hubble Heritage Team [AURA/STScI])

Orion Nebula, positioned 1,500 light-years away (see figure 5.4 on p. 87).

The Orion Nebula is barely visible to the naked eye as the middle "star" in the constellation's sword. It blocks out a section of the sky only as large as two Moon diameters. Astronomers would face a major obstacle, however, if the Orion Nebula were exchanged for the Tarantula. If the Tarantula Nebula sat as close to Earth as the Orion, it would fill nearly one-fourth of the night sky. It would also shower Earth with enough light to cast shadows. A sense of the difference becomes clearer through a side-by-side comparison

Figure 5.4. The Orion Nebula

The closest gaseous nebula to the solar system actively forming stars is the Orion Nebula. It is by far the brightest nebula in the sky. It appears as the "star" in the middle of Orion's sword. (Image courtesy of Corbis)

of the two nebulae (see figure 5.5 on p. 88). Again, in such circumstances, astronomers would have little or no knowledge of all the cosmic objects lying behind the 40-degree-wide nebula.

The words one of my grad school professors uttered one day amid a course on the structure of the Milky Way still echo in my mind: "What a wonder that we dwell in a galaxy in which we can see all its wonders!" Today, even more than back then, astronomers appreciate how superbly designed our galaxy is to permit the discovery of its multiple fine-tuned features, characteristics that make possible not only human existence but also our global high-tech civilization.

Dark Galaxy Clusters

Astronomers can also be glad that the Milky Way Galaxy sits in the darkest, or at least one of the darkest, locations in the universe where advanced physical life conceivably could exist. For advanced life to be possible, its galaxy must reside in a cluster of galaxies.

Figure 5.5. The Orion and Tarantula Nebulae to Scale

The above two images show how the Orion Nebula (left) and the Tarantula Nebula (right) would compare if both were the same distance from Earth. The images have been scaled for both size and brightness. (Orion Nebula: Image courtesy of Corbis; Tarantula Nebula: Image courtesy of NASA and the Hubble Heritage Team [AURA/STScI])

Otherwise, the galaxy could not absorb the mass of an adequate number of dwarf and subdwarf galaxies to maintain the kind of stable spiral structure required by advanced life.

Life in a cluster of galaxies poses substantial risks, however, for advanced life (see pp. 68–72). Unless the cluster takes on several highly fine-tuned characteristics, advanced life cannot survive. Extraordinary fine-tuning also is needed for astronomers to see much of what lies beyond their galaxy.

In the vast majority of clusters of galaxies, the galaxies are jammed tightly together with much of the cluster space dominated by giant and supergiant galaxies (see figure 4.4 and accompanying text). For such a galaxy cluster, an astronomer's view would be blocked by several adjacent galaxies that would fill large portions of the night sky. In the Milky Way Galaxy's cluster, the Local

Group, the galaxies are far apart (see figure 4.5). Furthermore, because the Local Group lacks any giant or supergiant galaxies and contains only two medium-sized galaxies (the Milky Way and Andromeda), astronomers can see all but a few Moon diameters' worth of the night sky.

Likewise, adjacent galaxy clusters and superclusters do little to block out the night sky. The closest significantly large cluster of galaxies is the Virgo cluster. If the Virgo cluster were much closer, it would present a major visibility barrier. However, if it were much farther away, astronomers would lack a large galaxy cluster to study in detail.

Just as there are superclusters of galaxies in the universe, there are also super-superclusters of galaxies and apparently super-super-superclusters of galaxies. The Local Group is distant enough from the center of the Virgo supercluster that the Virgo does not significantly impair astronomers' view. So, too, the Virgo supercluster is distant enough from the center of its super-supercluster (the Great Attractor) and its super-super-supercluster (the Monster Attractor) that astronomers on Earth have no trouble probing the depths of the heavens and mapping out in great detail the structure of the entire detectable universe.

Other Kinds of Darkness

Earth's dark location enables human observers to see both bright and dim objects through the darkness of what once seemed "empty space." However, as chapter 2 explains, both the bright and dim objects represent a miniscule fraction of all the stuff that makes up the universe (pp. 36–38). Virtually all the matter and energy in the universe can be described as dark. Imagine the painful glare if it weren't! And without that dark stuff, we wouldn't be here to discover it or be mystified by it.

To recap the numbers, dark energy makes up about 72 percent of the total content of the universe.[8] Of the remaining 28 percent, the majority (23 percent) is exotic dark matter. Exotic dark matter only weakly interacts with photons and thus emits no light. Ordinary dark matter—consisting of ordinary particles such as protons, neutrons, and electrons—constitutes slightly less than 4.2 percent of the universe. This ordinary kind of matter, such as the stuff our planet and human bodies are made of, emits light only when it's clumped together in bodies as big as stars. Otherwise, it's dark. Some 94 percent of it is dark. Only 0.27 percent of the total content of the universe emits any light at visual wavelengths.

Where Does Cosmic Darkness Reside?

While astronomers worked to figure out what the universe is made of, they became even more intrigued as to why all the dark stuff exists at all and exactly where it resides. As it turns out, the answers to these mysteries intertwine. When astronomers first accepted the reality of dark matter, they saw it as serving no important role for life's existence. A few years ago, however, when astronomers began to discern where the various kinds of darkness dwell, they discovered that its precise placement represents one of the features, actually a set of features, most amazingly fine-tuned for life's sake.

Swiss American astronomer Fritz Zwicky was the first to recognize that dark stuff dominates the universe and that its location plays a critical role in determining the structure of galaxies and galaxy clusters. In the 1940s he noted that the dynamics of galaxy clusters could only be kept stable if dark matter resides in and/or around those clusters in quantities far greater than the matter astronomers could then see. Not until the 1990s, though, did astronomers establish that exotic dark matter is indeed much more abundant than ordinary dark matter. And the confirmation of dark energy's existence took until the end of that decade.

Since the start of the twenty-first century, astronomers have achieved what many scientists once considered impossible. They have determined where the three different forms of cosmic darkness reside:

> *Dark energy* resides everywhere on the entire cosmic surface at the exact same level or strength. (All of the universe's matter and energy are confined to the cosmic surface.)

Exotic dark matter resides in far-out halos around large galaxies and galaxy clusters.

Ordinary dark matter resides in closer halos around galaxies of all types.

The locations of exotic and ordinary dark matter seem even more counterintuitive than turning your headlights down instead of up when you drive into a fogbank. Because of gravity, matter attracts matter. Therefore, matter tends to concentrate toward the center of any aggregate of mass. So we would expect matter to be most abundant at the core of a galaxy or galaxy cluster, not in the outer extremities. Yet in the case of both exotic dark matter and ordinary dark matter, astronomers observe the opposite.

Researchers have made considerable headway in understanding why ordinary dark matter resides predominantly in halos around all the galaxies. The largest stars ever to form took shape when the universe was just 365 million years old.[9] Such enormous stars burn up in a couple of million years or less. They go out with a bang as "hypernovae" explosions that erupt almost simultaneously with cataclysmic force. These hypernovae blow out virtually all the gas collected by gravity inside the emerging galaxies into halo-like structures that surround each galaxy.

Why exotic dark matter resides in even larger halos around huge galaxies and clusters of galaxies remains an enigma. This mystery likely will stay unsolved until astronomers and physicists discover the fundamental particles that make up exotic matter and identify the properties of these particles.

Physicists and astronomers have begun to understand, however, why these strange locations for ordinary and exotic dark matter are significant for life by applying a "what if" question: what if all or even a substantial quantity of the exotic and ordinary dark matter were centrally concentrated rather than distributed in halos? That concentration would force nearly all the ordinary matter (visible and dark) to collapse into the cores of galaxies. Massive galaxies would quickly gobble up the less massive galaxies, leading to even greater concentrations of matter. Star formation in the remaining galaxies would be extremely aggressive and concentrated, leading to the formation of hypermassive black holes in the core of each galaxy.

The central concentration of stars and black holes in each galaxy would make the formation of habitable planets impossible. That concentration would blast their environs with deadly radiation, making life doubly impossible. Needless to say, the light would be so intense as to rule out any possibility of astronomical observations.

Located where it is—with the masses, diameters, and structures as they are within the two different kinds of dark-matter halos— all this dark stuff supports the structure of spiral galaxies through time in such a way as to allow for the existence of at least one life-support planet. The quantities and distributions of the different forms of cosmic dark matter also permit observers on that one life-support planet to explore and map the structure of the universe and to trace its history back to its point of origin. The amazing details that have already emerged from that effort reveal many of the hidden purposes of the universe.

Signs of Design and Purpose

The very best locations and quantities of all the different forms of darkness to allow humans to observe all the wonders of the universe equate with the very best locations and quantities of the same forms of darkness to allow for the existence of a bountiful, beautiful home for humanity. Such a convergence would seem more than an accident. These multiple "coincidences" speak of supernatural intention.

The optimization of cosmic darkness and of Earth's location within the dark universe that sacrifices neither the material needs of human beings nor their capacity to gain knowledge about the universe reflects masterful engineering at a level far beyond human capability—and even imagination. It testifies of a supernatural, superintelligent, superpowerful, fully deliberate Creator.

Clearly, Someone wanted human beings to exist and thrive. Just as clearly, Someone wanted us to see all he had done in the universe. His purposes for human existence must be highly valuable. By studying the universe in all its detail—as the Creator apparently made sure we could—we have begun to discover and understand some of his purposes. And that quest continues.

Already enough has been discovered to answer some of the thorniest questions about why the universe is the way it is. Questions about cosmic decay, addressed in the next chapter, would likely be included in that group.

6

Why a Decaying Universe?

All cars break down, even the best of them. The older a vehicle gets, the more maintenance it requires, but eventually even the most beautifully restored models end up as scrap metal. Decay is an inescapable fact, and it applies to both living and nonliving things.

It's ironic that the same physical law that governs the decay process also makes engines work and physical life possible. The second law of thermodynamics, also known as the law of increasing entropy or simply the law of increasing decay, fundamentally has to do with the heat transfer from hot bodies to cold. That heat dissipation makes work and life possible.

The rate at which decay proceeds in the universe is extremely high.[1] That may seem bad, but it's not. If the rate of decay were any lower, galactic systems would trap radiation in such a manner that stars could not form. Starless galaxies would fill the universe. On the other hand, if the decay rate were slightly higher, no galactic systems would form at all.

The extreme predominance of decay, or heat dissipation, makes Earth a suitable home for physical life, especially for advanced life capable of launching a high-tech civilization. Decay also plays an essential role in explaining why the universe is the way it is. Insights into this role can be obtained by examining some of the less obvious but apparently negative aspects of decay, as well as its potent accelerant, dark energy.

Cosmic Heat Death

Who doesn't complain about how much work the battle against decay requires? British physicist William Thomson (known as Lord Kelvin) took such concerns to a whole new level in 1851–52 when he described the dire consequences looming in the second law of thermodynamics. He pointed out that the universal dissipation of mechanical energy would inevitably lead to a complete diffusion of heat, the cessation of all motion, the exhaustion of potential energy, and a universal state of death.[2]

This "heat death" of the universe follows from the simple fact that the flow of heat from hot bodies to cold bodies eventually brings every piece of matter in the universe to the exact same temperature. When everything registers an identical temperature, heat flow everywhere ceases. The universal cessation of heat flow implies the end of any possible performance of work, including such basic activities as respiration and digestion. The end of all work, then, spells the end of all physical life.

Only if the second law of thermodynamics could be reversed or proven less than a "law" would this heat death be avoidable. Paradoxically, without the constant and changeless operation of the second law of thermodynamics, physical life is impossible.

No Escape Clause

In the 1920s and 1930s, two other British mathematical physicists, Sir Arthur Eddington and Sir James Jeans, made the concept of cosmic heat death more widely known.[3] Thomson, Eddington, and Jeans, however, all developed their conclusions about the future state of the universe long before physicists and astronomers had acquired a high degree of certainty about the long-term stability of the physical laws or about the history and structure of the universe.

Many physicists during the first half of the twentieth century seriously questioned the stability of the assumptions about heat death. Most notably, Nobel laureate Robert Millikan, a strongly committed believer in God, vehemently objected to "the nihilistic doctrine" of an ultimate cosmic end of activity. His objection led to a valiant search for loopholes, such as speculations about the spontaneous replenishment of particles and/or energy "in the depths of space."[4]

Speculation about possible escapes from heat death ended when astronomers confirmed three facts:

1. The universe had a definite beginning in finite time.
2. The laws and constants of physics have been fixed since then.
3. The universe has been continually expanding since that creation event and will keep on expanding.

The discovery that dark energy dominates the dynamics of the universe confirms the ongoing cosmic expansion at an accelerating rate (see chapter 2, pp. 38–40). No reversal of this expansion or of the physical laws' operations is possible. There is no escape from the looming heat death for the universe or anything confined to it.

Time Line of Cosmic Consequences

Now that astronomers have determined the details of the origin, history, and structure of the universe and of the stability and constancy of the physical laws throughout cosmic history, they can calculate exactly how the heat-death scenario will unfold. Scientists can also determine how the different death events along the way will affect advanced life-forms, including human beings.

Though several astronomers have outlined the seemingly tragic narrative for the benefit of laypeople,[5] the *Astrophysical Journal* published a more detailed and rigorous account several years ago. Lawrence Krauss, chairman of the physics and astronomy department at Case Western Reserve University, coauthored along with colleague Glenn Starkman an article titled "Life, the Universe, and Nothing: Life and Death in an Ever-Expanding Universe." In it they calculate the future consequences of ever-accelerating cosmic expansion. They show that any kind of advanced physical life confined to the space-time dimensions of the cosmos must suffer an inevitable, irreversible, and complete dissipation of heat.[6]

With every passing year, the universe stretches out faster than it did the previous year, which hastens and exacerbates the consequences of the coming heat death. Krauss and Starkman demonstrated how this ever-increasing cosmic expansion rate, when projected far into the future, yields at least six deeply distressing consequences—each more serious than the one before. These results include:

1. Decreasing observability

Accelerating expansion, at its measured rate, implies that astronomers will increasingly see less of the universe and retain less of their capacity to explore cosmic history (see chapter 3, pp. 53–55). The reason is that all the stuff of the universe is confined to the surface of the universe. At any given rate of cosmic expansion, objects more widely separated will move away from each other at higher velocities than objects closer together. (An expanding balloon provides a good analogy. Dots scattered far apart on the surface of the balloon before it's blown up will, as the balloon fills with air, move away from one another more rapidly than will dots closer together.)

With the cosmic surface expanding at an accelerating rate, it is simply a matter of time before the objects farthest apart move away from each other at a velocity greater than the speed of light (see "Exceeding the Light-Speed Limit," chapter 3, p. 56). When that happens, light from one object will be unable to travel along the surface fast enough to reach the other object. It becomes permanently invisible. As the universe gets older, astronomers will increasingly lose their capacity to look back in time by observing distant objects.

As more and more of the cosmic space surface relative to Earth continues to stretch at speeds greater than the velocity of light, less of the universe will be visible to Earth-bound observers and to their space-based telescopes. Distant galaxies and in time even the stars in the Milky Way will disappear from view. Eventually the Sun will recede from Earth at a speed that exceeds light's velocity, permanently separating us from the Sun's heat and light. The capacity of humans to observe the universe and learn about its past history will inexorably diminish to the point of complete ignorance about its origin, history, dynamics (including expansion), and structure.

2. Cessation of star burning

Long before the Sun ceases to be visible (due to accelerating cosmic expansion), stars throughout the entire universe, including the Sun, will burn out. This outcome is a direct consequence of the universe's extremely high rate of decay.

Already, after just 13.73 billion years of cosmic history, most of the gas-and-dust pockets from which stars form have been expended. In fact, star formation continues in only a small percentage of present-day galaxies (see figure 6.1, p. 100). So as space increasingly stretches, what little gas and dust remains becomes more widely dispersed—so dispersed that eventually star formation everywhere in the universe will cease altogether.

Like car engines, stars burn for only a limited time before they run out of fuel. The bigger the star, the faster its fuel burns, just as larger car engines consume fuel more rapidly than smaller ones.

Due to the very high rate of decay that results from the laws of physics and the characteristics of the universe, stars burn up in a relatively short period of time. The largest stars extinguish in only a few million years. Smaller stars, similar in size to the Sun, can continue burning for almost 10 billion years. The smallest stars that can possibly burn (a star's mass must exceed 8 percent of the Sun's mass to ignite nuclear burning in the star's core) may be able to burn nuclear fuel for nearly 100 billion years, but no longer.

**Figure 6.1. The Core of the Orion Nebula, a Region of Active Star
    Formation**

The Milky Way Galaxy is one of only a small percentage of galaxies that still forms new stars. Such
star formation, however, is limited to several dense molecular clouds embedded in the spiral arms
and the nucleus of the Milky Way Galaxy. In this image over a dozen newborn stars can be seen
emerging from their gas-dust cocoons. (Image courtesy of NASA-HQ-GRIN)

Besides the highly dissipated and by now very cool radiation
(–270.4°C or –454.8°F) left over from the cosmic beginning event,
stars provide virtually all the light and heat in the universe. As
more and more stars burn out and as all star formation grinds to
a halt, the universe will grow dramatically darker and heat flow
everywhere will drop precipitously. That drop will then trigger
other serious calamities.

3. Decreasing knowledge

Today knowledge is increasing at a phenomenal rate. In some disciplines, the knowledge base doubles every four to five years. This increase in learning has been going on now for so many generations that most people take it for granted. We tend to presume it will continue indefinitely. However, as Krauss and Starkman pointed out in their article, the physical realities of the universe dictate that this knowledge accumulation will eventually reach a limit and then reverse.

The accumulation and retrieval of knowledge—whether through the human intellect, a supercomputer, or some exotic artificial intelligence—requires work. It demands the dissipation of heat through some type of organism or machine. The catastrophic drop in the heat dissipation rate that results from the burning out of all stars implies a cataclysmic drop in the rate at which knowledge can be accumulated because heat flow is essential to gaining, sustaining, and retrieving stored knowledge.

An optimally advanced civilization, assuming it survives long enough, will at some point reach a peak level of information gathering and thereafter will experience a decline down to zero. Beyond that time it will begin to lose knowledge at an increasingly rapid rate. In other words, humanity or any other possibly existing intelligent species in the universe is condemned by the laws of physics and the properties of the universe eventually to become more and more ignorant until they know nothing at all.

4. Cessation of protein folding and metabolism

All basic life functions depend on precisely specified protein structures and complex metabolic reactions. The assembly of these protein structures, through the linking together of certain sequences of amino acids and the folding of these amino acid chains into specified three-dimensional shapes, requires a certain level of heat flow. As cosmic expansion continues to accelerate, a time will come when that heat flow level will no longer be available. Protein production will cease and so will the metabolic reactions they govern. At this theoretical point, all physical life must come to an end—not just on Earth but everywhere in the cosmos.

5. End of consciousness

The universe will eventually expand so rapidly as to become devoid of life. As physical life comes to an end, the universe becomes permanently devoid of any thinking, contemplation, awareness, and emotion. Even if consciousness were reduced to mere quantum mechanical computational machines (machines with the lowest possible energy demands), that kind of "thinking" would eventually come to a halt in a universe that continually expands at an accelerating rate.

This sterilization of the universe and, along with it, the end of all activity that could be described as consciousness would likely occur long before the cosmic expansion rate brings about a theoretical end to all metabolic reactions and all protein assembly and folding. A few metabolic reactions could conceivably continue to occur in the temperature and heat-flow conditions of a universe in which all the stars have burned out, but most could not. Given that life requires the operation of multiple simultaneous metabolic functions as well as the activities of many different kinds of protein and replicating (DNA) molecules, the end of all physical life in the universe from this perspective alone cannot be postponed much beyond the era of star burning.

Even if the universe could somehow escape the decay effects of entropy and dark energy, a fundamental limit on the duration of life and consciousness in the universe emerges from the inevitability of proton decay (see "Proton Decay: A Fundamental Limit on Physical Life," p. 103). Apparently not even protons can last forever. At the decay rate physicists calculate, sometime before the universe reaches ten thousand trillion trillion trillion years old, all its protons—and neutrons—will disintegrate. A universe without protons and neutrons is a universe without atoms and molecules. Without atoms and molecules, physical life can't exist.

Proton Decay: A Fundamental Limit on Physical Life

Though proton decay has yet to be directly observed, physicists are convinced it occurs. They are convinced because matter predominates antimatter in the universe.

For the big bang creation event to favor the production of matter over antimatter, some form of "symmetry breaking" must have occurred during the creation of fundamental particles. All these forms imply proton decay. Most show that a proton decays into a positron (an antielectron) and a neutral pion, and the pion immediately decays into high-energy photons (gamma rays).

Free neutrons, that is, neutrons outside of atomic nuclei, also decay. Their half-life is 10.2 minutes (in other words, half the free neutrons in any given sample will decay within 10.2 minutes). A neutron breaks down into a proton, an electron, and an antineutrino. Then the proton decays (as described above).

Most particle physicists' models estimate the half-life of protons to be about a trillion trillion trillion years. Though a definitive decay rate measurement exceeds the capability of existing particle detectors, that measurement seems within reach of the next generation of detectors, such as Japan's proposed Hyper-Kamiokande.

---

6. The end of meaning

If "the cosmos is all that is or ever was or ever will be," to repeat Carl Sagan's claim,[7] then the fact that it results in the extermination of all life and consciousness also extinguishes the possibility of ultimate hope, purpose, or destiny. The implications of centuries of research into the physics of the cosmos are dismal: life confined to a continually accelerating, ever-expanding space-time matrix possesses no possibility for lasting contribution, enduring legacy, or ultimate meaning.

The one ray of hope to which humanity may cling—the possibility that astronomers might not be correct in their observations and measurements of this newly discovered dark energy—was dashed by the research findings of the seven years following Krauss and Starkman's article. At the time of publication in 2000, only a year had passed since the initial discovery of dark energy, which not only accelerates cosmic decay but guarantees it cannot be reversed.[8] Its existence had been detected by only a single measuring method. Since then, however, astronomers have successfully detected dark energy by seven additional means. Each one established not only that dark energy exists but also that it is the dominant component of the universe. In addition, these detections showed that dark energy density is most likely constant throughout cosmic history.

The most accurate of the detections, based on the Wilkinson Microwave Anisotropy Probe team's measurements of the cosmic background radiation, showed that dark energy comprises 72.1 ± 1.5 percent of the total stuff of the universe.[9] That level of precision (indicated by the small error bar) virtually closes the case.

If the universe really is "all that is," as Sagan, naturalists, and secular humanists claim, then what anyone does with his or her life—whether a person lives or dies, loves or hates, gains knowledge or remains ignorant—carries no ultimate significance or purpose whatsoever.

Going against the Grain

In one important respect Krauss and Starkman's article and conclusions struck a mighty blow against naturalism and secular humanism. Their calculations essentially falsified the latest doctrinal pronouncements (published in 2002) of the Council for Secular Humanism. In part, its Statement of Principles declares:

- We deplore efforts . . . to seek to explain the world in supernatural terms and to look outside nature for salvation.
- We are citizens of the universe.
- We affirm humanism as a realistic alternative to theologies of despair.
- We believe in optimism rather than pessimism, hope rather than despair, learning in the place of dogma, truth instead of ignorance.[10]

Ironically, if the universe is *it*, as the Council asserts, then the pessimism and despair they vehemently deplore represents the only reasonable response to reality. The truth we have learned is the inevitability of ignorance.

The Magnitude of an *If*

On the other hand, *if* the universe is not the sum total of reality, then life may actually hold some meaning. *If* the paradise, heaven, or utopia many people long for does exist somewhere beyond this universe, then humanity's hope, purpose, and destiny may be rooted in reality after all. Of course, the physical laws and dimensions of such a place would need to be different.

As the data reveals, a one-universe scenario offers the human race nothing to live for. Decay processes, also described as heat-transfer laws, that play a vital role in life's existence also lead ultimately to life's cessation.

Some astrophysicists have proposed a multiverse (or multiple-universe scenario) as a way around this conclusion, but others point out that it offers no hope either. Even if the cosmic creation event generated multiple physical universes, Einstein's relativity principles come into play. As soon as conditions mature enough to permit the existence of physical observers, from that time onward it becomes impossible for the space-time manifold or surface of the observers' universe to make physical contact with the space-time surface of any other possibly existing physical universe. In other words, even in a multiverse, physical observers would remain confined to their particular universe, a universe that eventually becomes lifeless through the inevitability of decay.

Yet people do hope. They have an innate sense of purpose, a sense of destiny. Not just a few people but all people to one degree or another. Does it make sense to assume that everyone suffers from the same irrational, inexplicable delusion, or is there a rational, testable basis within a decaying universe to embrace hope and a sense of life's meaningfulness?

If sound scientific support can be found for the reality of ultimate hope, purpose, and destiny, then:

1. Sagan's creedal assertion that the cosmos is "all that is"[11] must be false,
2. human beings may have access to a realm beyond the physical cosmos, and
3. the purpose behind the law of decay most likely extends beyond provision of an environment in which, for at least a relatively brief time, protein folding, metabolism, learning, and star burning can occur.

Some of the scientific evidence on which these statements rest appears in the previous chapters, especially chapters 4 and 5, but much more could be given. Chapter 7 shows why, from a scientific perspective, something beyond this familiar cosmos must exist.

7

Why a Realm beyond This One?

Everyone at RTB drives a traditional car except for Marj. She's entered a brand-new realm of automotive experience—the hybrid. Her Prius not only departs from the tradition of complete dependence on an internal combustion engine but also comes with an onboard computer that teaches the driver how to achieve superior gas mileage.

Once while I was in Denver, an RTB chapter member loaned me a Prius. The scientist in me quickly appreciated its technology, especially all the ways it showed how to take advantage of the operating efficiencies of its battery, braking system, and gasoline engine. Within a couple of days I learned how to squeeze 55 miles or more out of every gallon burned in a combination of city, highway, and mountain driving.

For decades, no one even dreamed of a practical auto world based on anything other than the internal combustion engine— one that accomplished purposes beyond the familiar. So too it took decades for astronomers to consider the reality and practical possibility of a realm beyond the cosmos. But the recognition that our universe cannot by itself provide humans with ultimate hope, purpose, and destiny (see chapter 6, pp. 97–104), coupled with several new lines of scientific evidence for the existence of another realm (see descriptive list, pp. 108–118), stirs new hope.

Temporal and Spatial Coincidences

Accelerating cosmic expansion implies that if we humans had arrived on the scene much later than 13.73 billion years after the universe began, we would see only a fraction of cosmic history (see chapter 3, pp. 54–55). Humans couldn't have come much earlier, either, or their home would not have been ready and their view of cosmic history would have been quite limited (see chapters 2 and 3, pp. 29–32 and 53–56). It turns out that humans arrived right in the middle of the one narrow time window when we can live well *and* see the entirety of cosmic history.

This special timing of humanity's appearance in cosmic history represents either a caused, *purposeful* concurrence or an unexpected coincidence. The skeptic in each of us says, "Improbable things do happen." Dozens of examples jump to mind—the occasional golfer sinks a hole in one, old friends cross paths while running to catch flights at O'Hare, a meteorite crashes through the roof and lands on the living room floor as a couple watches a disaster movie about an asteroid collision.

One such event may not carry much significance. But when simultaneous "coincidences" multiply, the "random accident" interpretation grows less and less plausible and reaches a point at which it must be abandoned. The fact that humanity pops up in the just-right time window for astronomers to observe the universe and all of its history *and* in virtually the only possible location within the vastness of the cosmos where these features can be seen (see chapter 5, pp. 79–89) lends credence to the idea that Someone wanted the cosmos to be observed for a particular reason.

Within the context of the laws of physics that govern the universe, both the location of humanity's home within the cosmos (see chapter 4, pp. 65–72, and chapter 5, pp. 79–89) and the timing of humanity's appearance in cosmic history (see chapter 3, pp. 44–52) combine to maximize the bounty, prosperity, and technology specifically beneficial for humanity.

Four simultaneous space-time optimizations for human benefit indicate purpose, not chance. Someone planned and prepared for humans to exist and thrive at this unique time and locale in the universe. Someone must have intended human observers to see all that was done on their behalf throughout the past 13.73 billion years of cosmic history and throughout the observable universe of 50 billion trillion stars. These indicators of purpose for humanity imply that ongoing research should uncover additional examples of our perfect positioning in time and space.

Providential Time Windows

Innumerable conditions must be exquisitely optimized for the support of humanity and of civilization. Many of them are highly time variable. Evidence showing that a wide variety of independent conditions all reached optimality during the identical narrow epoch when human beings appeared on the cosmic and terrestrial scene testifies of supernatural design and purpose rather than mere coincidence. A few examples (among many) bring into focus the precisely aligned optimizations:

1. Earth's rotation rate

Powerful tidal forces exerted on Earth by the Sun and even more so by the Moon slowed the planet's rotation rate from two to three hours per day (at the Moon's formation) to the current twenty-four. This slowing of Earth's rotation rate has taken 4.5 billion years, thus far, and continues still. In another 100 million years, Earth days will last twenty-five hours.

When the rotation rate was more rapid, rainfall was less evenly distributed over the planet's surface. Hurricanes, tornadoes, and storms were more targeted on certain geographical regions. Less heat transferred from the tropics to the poles, which meant less biomass and less biodiversity in high-latitude regions.[1] Less nighttime cooling meant many plant and tree species were less able to produce what the human economy requires.

On the other hand, as the rate slows to twenty-five hours, temperature differences between day and night will become more extreme. In several parts of the world, humans and other species of life already have difficulty surviving these temperature highs and lows without the benefit of artificial heating and air-conditioning. A longer rotation rate will also significantly disturb Earth's rainfall distribution patterns. Humans live at the ideal rotation rate epoch in Earth's history.

2. Fossil fuels

The decayed bodies of creatures buried during or soon after the Cambrian explosion (about 543 million years ago) made the largest contribution to Earth's petroleum reserves. While the transformation of these buried remains (via geochemistry) into usable petroleum takes time, given too much time bacteria in the crust will turn the petroleum into natural gas. Likewise, the formation of reservoir structures in Earth's crust for the collection and storage of petroleum requires certain geological developments that take specific periods of time. However, with too much time, tectonic activity will cause cracks to form in the sealer rocks. Such cracks mean petroleum loss through leaks.

The optimal time for petroleum production perfectly matches the optimal time for reservoir structure formation and the storage of petroleum in those structures. These circumstances coincide perfectly with the timing of humanity's appearance on Earth. In other words, humans are living on Earth at the optimal moment for petroleum exploitation. The conditions for coal formation and storage are also exacting and equally optimal in their timing for the benefit of humans and civilization.

3. Solar stability

When stars like the Sun reach "middle age" (as ours has), they achieve maximum stability. In the years before and after middle age, flaring activity is greater (see figure 3.2). More frequent and violent flares release radiation with the potential to harm advanced life, particularly those creatures with long life spans.

The Sun currently burns with the greatest consistency possible. This exceptional stability began about 50,000 years ago and will continue for another 50,000 years.[2] The Sun's radiation profile today perfectly suits the requirements for sustaining global high-technology human civilization.

4. Solar luminosity

A star's brightness varies considerably during its hydrogen-burning phase (see figure 3.3). During the past 3 billion years, the Sun's luminosity has increased by about 15 percent, enough to destroy life if not for the carefully orchestrated introduction of the just-right species at the just-right population levels at the just-right times. These layers of life removed greenhouse gases (primarily carbon dioxide and water) from the atmosphere in just the right amounts to compensate for the Sun's heat-producing luminosity increase. More than 3 billion years of this ongoing process loaded Earth's crust with a wealth of biodeposits, the resources humans needed for the rapid launch and ongoing support of global civilization.

In other words, humans arrived on the terrestrial scene at the perfect moment, from the biological/biodeposit perspective. The human era coincides with the ideal surface temperature and the ideal abundance and diversity of plants to support civilization. But these ideal conditions won't last indefinitely. The Sun's increasing brightness will one day (within several million years) reach a point at which this temperature balancing act can no longer be sustained. The required removal of greenhouse gases (to keep all life sufficiently cool) will leave plants, on which our livelihood largely depends, without adequate carbon dioxide for efficient photosynthesis. The decline of plant life eventually will take a devastating toll on animal life, especially on the quality and survivability of human life. These discoveries tell us that humans appeared on Earth at the optimal solar moment, which coincides with the optimal biodeposit and photosynthetic moment.

5. Perfect eclipses

Only when the Sun's diameter exactly matched the Moon's diameter as seen from Earth's surface did perfect eclipses become possible. Because the Moon continually spirals away from Earth, this matchup takes place within a certain time window. A few million years ago, the Moon's diameter was larger than the Sun's. Only a few million years from now, that diameter will be smaller.

Because humanity's arrival in the solar system coincides with this perfect eclipse window, people living before the advent of modern technology were able to determine the geometry and the scale of Earth's solar system. They could also use the timing of solar eclipses to calibrate their calendars and maintain accurate historical records. Perfect solar eclipses have allowed modern researchers to study the Sun's corona and discover its characteristics. Perfect solar eclipses also helped astrophysicists confirm general relativity soon after Einstein first proposed the theory.[3]

6. Plate tectonics

The human era also coincides with the best seismic moment in Earth's history. Powerful tectonic forces played the primary role in lifting Earth's continental landmasses above the surface of its early global ocean (4 to 4.5 billion years ago). Several billion years of plate tectonic activity grew continents and islands to the point where they now comprise 29 percent of Earth's surface (see figure 3.5). Research shows that this is the ideal landmass coverage for sustaining a large, globally distributed, high-tech human population.[4] Not only is the current land area ideal, but so are the shapes, elevation patterns, orientations, and relative positions of the continents, islands, and oceans. All appear to be optimal for the sake of human civilization.

Plate tectonics can be destructive too. Most of the energy-driving plate movement comes from the decay of long-lived radiometric isotopes in the Earth's interior. If the human race had arrived earlier on the terrestrial scene, this radiation exposure would have been deadly and volcanic and earthquake activity too intense. A later arrival would have meant living without the benefit of abundant nutrient-rich volcanic soils.

Just Right for Humankind

Many other conditions necessary for human existence and beneficial to quality of life are also time critical.[5] The fact that these features, the known number of which continues to grow, all converge simultaneously at the moment human beings arrive on the planet defies realistic probability. One favorable time window's alignment with even one other window might be considered an astounding coincidence. But the lineup of so many independent time windows with the brief human moment on the cosmic calendar speaks powerfully of purpose.

This conclusion is one component of what the scientific community has labeled the "anthropic principle"—the observation that the universe appears to have been engineered for the specific benefit of the human species. The currently calculated level of this fine-tuning—and the question of whether it targeted humanity or life in general—will be described in more detail in chapter 8.

So Much Invested for Such a Short Time

In 1983 a British mathematician, Brandon Carter, introduced what he called the "anthropic principle inequality" to the scientific world. Carter took note of the fact that several billion years is the minimum time required for the universe to expand and develop sufficiently to allow for the existence of the human race or a similarly advanced species. Yet, according to his calculations, the maximum time window in which the cosmos can possibly sustain such a species amounts to less than a few million years.[6] In other words, it took a very long time to prepare the universe to sustain humans for a relatively short time.

Physicists John Barrow and Frank Tipler demonstrated in 1986 that the inequality is far more extreme than Carter figured. They estimated that global human civilization—something more than just a few low-population people groups existing in one or two regions using Stone Age–type tools—could last no more than 41,000 years.[7] According to their calculations, this limit would apply to any physical intelligent species with a sophisticated global civilization living anywhere in the universe.[8]

Barrow and Tipler noted that the laws of physics, the characteristics of the universe, and the properties of life would all contribute to this brevity of duration for advanced life. Other factors include the Earth's rotation rate, fossil fuel supplies, solar stability, solar luminosity, and plate tectonics, as well as those characteristics discussed in chapter 3 (see pp. 44–52). Additional limitations apply to affluent high-tech civilizations. These include declining birthrates, increasing genetic disorders, environmental catastrophes, sociopolitical upheaval, and more.[9]

The bottom line of these calculations is that the maximum time window for the existence of a global, civilized, highly technological species of life is 335,000 times narrower than the minimum time required to ready the physical environment for that species. Furthermore, that preparation involves so many intricate details intertwined with such exquisite fine-tuning and timing that only one reasonable conclusion emerges: the Creator of such an environment must possess unfathomable power, genius, resources, and above all else, purpose. That high purpose most apparently involves humans.

An analogy helps bring home the point of Carter's anthropic principle inequality. The average wedding ceremony lasts only briefly considering the amount of time, planning, and money it requires. A couple and perhaps their parents often invest large amounts of resources for an extremely short event. But they consider these resources well spent, given the event's high significance. Likewise, given that it costs the material resources of the entire universe and the investment of 13.73 billion years of time to support humanity and its civilization for only a few tens of thousands of years, the human species indeed must have immense worth and purpose.

In the movie *Contact*, based on Carl Sagan's novel, lead actress Jodie Foster and others repeatedly proclaim that the universe is a terrible waste if humans are alone in it. That may be true if humans are really alone (see chapter 6, pp. 104–06). But are we? The universe is far from a waste if the Creator endowed humans with a destiny that extends beyond the universe itself (see chapter 12, pp. 184–92).

Drive for Preservation

In the classic science fiction movie *2001: A Space Odyssey*, supercomputer HAL boasted a self-preservation subroutine (software that preserved the operation of the computer and protected it from outside influences intent on crippling its capability). I saw the movie shortly after its release in 1969. As one of the more prolific computer programmers at the University of Toronto, I walked out of the theater afterward naively presuming that by the end of the twentieth century, self-preservation subroutines would be a common feature of computer software.

Now, well into the twenty-first century, computer programmers are not even close to achieving a self-preservation subroutine. This situation persists in spite of computer hardware and software advances once unimaginable.

While no human programmer has been able to design a self-preservation subroutine for a computer, such "software" does exist in every living organism. Every life-form has a powerful internal drive to preserve its own life and that of its offspring.

Evolutionary theory claims this drive arose as a result of natural selection. Individuals with the strongest inclination for self-preservation would have the greatest likelihood to survive. However, this assertion does not answer the question of how this drive developed in the first place. It only offers a possible mechanism for selecting out *strong* drives for self-preservation from those at weaker levels.

Given the challenges today's computer programmers face in attempting to develop self-preservation software for mere computers, it seems reasonable to conclude that the causal Agent behind this drive in organisms must be at least somewhat more intelligent than today's best computer programmers. And just as computer programmers encode each program they write to achieve specific purposes, so also the causal Agent must have held specific intentions for his deliberate encoding of the self-preservation subroutines in all life-forms.

The Creator's investment in Earth's life is far from trivial. Life itself in all its complexity, diversity, and abundance demands an enormous outlay. That scientists still can't assemble even the simplest life-form in the lab from scratch (from nonorganic compounds), let alone make it live, preserve its life, and sustain life for billions of years, testifies to the level of the Creator's investment—and involvement.[10] This observation leads to an obvious conclusion: if the Creator put so much into creating and sustaining human life, then it must have an ultimate purpose.

Unique Human Drives

People, like all life-forms, are endowed with a powerful drive to maximize the longevity and the quality of their lives. Unlike all other species, however, humans possess certain drives that may, at times, supersede their desire for self-preservation. Unique to the human species, these powerful drives focus on discerning the meaning of life and achieving an ultimate, enduring destiny.

In some individuals, this drive manifests itself early, but often it emerges later, in midlife or beyond. Even people whose days and nights focus largely on the struggle to survive dream of a better life, and it keeps them going. Those who grow up in the better life tend to aim for the "good life," intent on achieving greater wealth, comfort, and pleasure. Then, at some point, the quest for something else takes hold. Conscious decisions are made to trade ease and sometimes even longevity for that which holds a different kind of value not only in the present but also in a realm beyond this one.

For some the drive toward hope, purpose, and destiny is so powerful it doesn't wait for a midlife crisis. Instead these individuals purposely seek out vocations that give their lives meaning right from the start. Or they choose occupations that give them the resources of wealth and/or time to devote to spiritual and humanitarian enterprises. Many people willingly choose a harder life, even a shorter life, to gain a sense of fulfillment—the fulfillment of an ultimately significant destiny.

Again, evolutionary theory says this powerful human impetus to seek life's purpose and eternal destiny arises from naturalistic processes, but from what source? This speculation rests on zero evidence. No predecessors left behind any indication of an interest in or capability to pursue such a thing. *Homo sapiens sapiens* (modern man) is the only bipedal primate species for which any undisputed evidence of the drive to seek more than physical survival and well-being exists.

Thus far, evolutionists have been unable to demonstrate any development or evolution of these drives within the human species. Humans living thousands and tens of thousands of years ago evidently manifested these motivations at the same levels as do people today.[11]

Where, then, does this strong desire come from? Why is it that the vast majority of the world's people—regardless of education, economics, politics, technology, and geography—believe in some kind of God?[12] Why do people the world over, including many scientists, persistently believe in a reality they cannot see and believe in an afterlife? Why do most people engage in some form of worship? If natural causes cannot explain this trait's origin, then it seems both reasonable and probable to conclude that it came from something or Someone beyond the natural realm. To put it another way, why would a Creator who demonstrates care and bountiful provision for humanity place such drives within the human spirit if no possibility for ultimate purpose and destiny exists?

Greater Reasons

There are many reasons for the belief that humanity's sense of hope and ultimate destiny are rooted in reality. The fact that this cosmos by itself cannot explain our most basic and utterly unique human desires represents just one. Perhaps the most significant reason of all pertains to the exquisite manner in which the physical laws of the universe serve to limit the expression of human evil and to prepare willing individuals for life in a realm where evil does not exist. Evidence that this divine purpose is at work in the cosmos cannot be adequately explained in a few paragraphs or even a single chapter. Two chapters in this book, chapters 12 and 13, are devoted to the subject, but they only begin to scratch the surface.

Some simpler, more rigorous demonstrations of the existence of a realm beyond the cosmos arise from Einstein's general relativity theorems and from certain applications of the anthropic principle. These demonstrations are described in chapter 11.

But first two major questions in a running scientific debate need to be addressed: (1) must the universe be designed by a supernatural being, and (2) if the universe, Milky Way Galaxy, and solar system were indeed designed, were they intended for life in general or for humans and their civilization in particular? The next chapter describes the latest efforts to answer these questions.

8

Why This Particular Planet, Star, Galaxy, and Universe?

No one at RTB owns the perfect car. Such a vehicle doesn't likely exist. One employee, however, seems a bit happier with his car than the rest of us. Ken drives a rebuilt Miata convertible that he sees as just right.

The Miata's ability to take corners without slowing appeals to Ken's inner race car driver. He enjoys even more feeling the sunshine while driving with the top down. Good gas mileage is another benefit. But perhaps what Ken likes best is how the Miata supports his hobby of restoring old homes. Ladders, lumber, and long-handled tools fit snugly against the floorboard, rest across the front seat, and extend out over the back. With the top down, Ken can haul stuff that is longer than the car. For Ken, the Miata comes close to perfection.

During the past several years of research, scientists have gathered a substantial body of evidence showing that the universe, the Milky Way Galaxy, the solar system, and Earth are, or at least have been, an essentially perfect vehicle for humanity. Though each astronomical component manifests features that may initially seem strange or out of place, in the context of humanity's needs, each characteristic is just right.

Echoes of Goldilocks

Scientists commonly define the anthropic principle as the premise that life's presence places many constraints on the physical features and historical development of the universe. Not much attention has yet been devoted to considering how dramatically these constraints multiply if that life is to survive millions or billions of years as opposed to a few months or years. Even less attention has been given to how much more they must be multiplied for the sake of human life as compared to unicellular life.

Previous chapters describe how the universe's size, mass, age, and distribution of matter must be fine-tuned to allow life to exist. Some sections focus specifically on the fine-tuning for humanity and advanced civilization, including humanity's opportunity to observe the entire extent and history of the cosmos.

Such fine-tuning certainly suggests that the universe may have been designed not just for any kind of life but for human life in particular. This idea can be more rigorously tested and established through more detailed comparisons of the fine-tuning required for the support of the following life-forms:

1. ephemeral simple life (unicellular life that survives for 90 days or less)
2. permanent simple life (unicellular life that persists for 3 billion years or more)
3. intelligent physical life (human beings or their functional equivalent)
4. intelligent physical life capable of launching and sustaining a global high-tech civilization

If the fine-tuning differences dramatically increase with the complexity of successive categories, and if the fine-tuning required for the fourth category is extreme at all levels of cosmic structure (laws of physics, universe as a whole, cluster of galaxies, galaxy, planetary system, star, planet, moon, surface of the planet, and life on the planet's surface), then it is reasonable to conclude that the universe exists for the specific purpose of providing a bountiful home for human beings and for equipping them with the necessary resources to launch and maintain a global high-tech civilization. That conclusion can be put to an additional test by determining the comparative degree to which evidence for the fine-tuning demands of the fourth category increase in relation to the others.

The Case for Fine-Tuning Grows

For more than twenty years, with assistance from RTB staff and volunteer scientists, I have been cataloguing evidences of fine-tuning for the survival and support of various kinds of life. Such classification spectacularly demonstrates that the more scientists learn about the laws of physics and the structure and substructures of the universe, the more evidence they compile in support of the conclusion that the universe was designed to make physical life—in all four categories—possible.

First, table 8.1 (see p. 122) compiled by RTB scientists, illustrates how that evidence has accumulated from research into the laws of physics and the gross features of the universe. Second, table 8.2 (see p. 122) offers the same kind of illustration based on research into the features of the Virgo supercluster, the Local Group, the Milky Way Galaxy, the solar system, and Earth. From 1995 to 2006, scientific evidence of the fine-tuning required for life's benefit became roughly a trillion trillion trillion trillion times stronger with each succeeding year's research. Such mounting evidence for fine-tuning shouts loudly that life must be more than a cosmic accident. The universe and its substructures must have been engineered to make physical life possible. (See table 8.3, p. 123 and "Must the Design Be Supernatural?" p. 124)

Third, table 8.4 augments the 2006 fine-tuning data (presented in table 8.2) by showing how the fine-tuning numbers decrease or increase depending on the complexity of the life-forms considered. Specifically, it shows the number of fine-tuned characteristics required for the support of each of three categories of life: ephemeral simple life, permanent simple life, and intelligent physical life capable of launching and sustaining a global high-technology civilization.

TABLE 8.1

Cosmic Features That Must Be Fine-Tuned
for Any Physical Life to Exist

Date	Features Observed
1988	15
1991	17
1995	26
1998	34
2001	41
2002	47
2004	77
2005	93
2006	140

For a descriptive list with literature citations for these specific characteristics, see appendix C, part 1, "Fine-Tuning for Life in the Universe," pp. 213–14.

TABLE 8.2

Galactic and Terrestrial Features That Must Be Fine-Tuned
to Support Permanent Simple Life

Year	Fine-tuned Features Observed	Probability of Finding Within the Observable Universe a Life-Supportable Body with These Features
1995	41	10^{-31}
2000	128	10^{-144}
2002	202	10^{-217}
2004	322	10^{-282}
2006	676	10^{-556}

For a descriptive list with literature citations of the fine-tuned characteristics and their respective probabilities, see appendix C, part 3, "Probability Estimates for the Features Required by Various Life-Forms," pp. 213–14. The probabilities take into account that the observable universe may contain 10 billion trillion planets and the fine-tuning degree for many features is dependent on the fine-tuning degree of other features.

TABLE 8.3

Fine-Tuned Features at Various Size Scales
That Support Advanced Life

Size Scale	Fine-tuned Features Observed	Probability of Finding One Such Life-Support System or Body
Universe	140	*
Galaxy cluster	99	10^{-53}
Galaxy	200	10^{-135}
Planetary system	137	10^{-112}
Star	140	10^{-108}
Moon	27	10^{-16}
Planet	268	10^{-281}
Planet's surface	137	10^{-106}
Planet's life	159	10^{-390}

*Note: Only this one universe is observable.

TABLE 8.4

Detailed Breakdown of Evidence for Fine-Tuning (as of 2006)

Life-Form	Fine-tuned Features Observed	Probability of Finding a Life-Supportable Body
Briefly existing bacteria	501	10^{-311}
Permanent bacteria	676	10^{-556}
High-tech humans	824	$10^{-1,050}$

For a descriptive list with literature citations of the different observed fine-tuned characteristics and their respective probabilities for the four different kinds of life, see appendix C, part 4, "Probability Estimates on Different Size Scales for the Features Required by Advanced Life," p. 214.

According to the research data, an astronomical body capable of supporting human beings and equipping them to launch and sustain a global high-technology civilization demands at least 10^{700} times more fine-tuning precision than is necessary for support of ephemeral simple life. To put this number (10^{700}) into perspective, the total number of protons and neutrons in the entire observable universe amounts to 10^{79}.

Must the Design Be Supernatural?

Many atheists and agnostics attempt to sidestep the compelling evidence for a purposeful design of the universe by appealing to an extreme form of the "multiverse" theory (see p. 105 for a brief explanation). While conceding that the universe is exquisitely fine-tuned to make life possible, they claim no God is necessary to explain the fine-tuning because beyond this universe an infinite number of other universes might possibly exist. Assuming the infinite number of universes all possess different characteristics, they argue that our universe's extremely fine-tuned characteristics arose by pure chance.

The problems with such an appeal are many and severe.[1] For example, on whatever volume scale researchers make their observations—the universe, galaxy cluster, galaxy, planetary system, planet, planetary surface, cell, atom, fundamental particle, or string—the evidence for extreme fine-tuning for life's sake, and in particular for humanity's benefit, persists (see table 8.3, pp. 122–23, for a summary and appendix C, pp. 213–14, for details).

What's more, the degree of design observed in a particular volume scale is proportional to the researcher's technological capability to measure the design there. Given that everywhere astronomers *can* measure design they *see* design, and given that the degree of design they measure is proportional to their capacity to detect and measure the design, it seems unreasonable (or disingenuous) to discount all that evidence by appealing to that which can never be detected or measured.

Such a dramatic difference compels the conclusion that the entire universe and all it contains exists and has been exquisitely designed for the purpose of making possible a global high-tech human civilization. Such a conclusion implies enormous significance and high purposes for the human species and their civilization. The next five chapters are devoted to deciphering at least some of them.

9

Why Believe the Bible?

Last year when two cars and a bicycle no longer covered the transportation needs of my four-driver household, I began shopping for the least expensive, most gas-efficient car I could find. My search led to a used Scion xA. My wife, Kathy, liked it, and we bought it despite one drawback: the previous owner had lost the owner's manual. After struggling to find such simple things as the button to unlock the passenger doors and puzzling over the CD player, we ordered a new manual.

The book came with a plain cover, no picture or words to identify the model and year to which it applied. So how could we know it was the right one?

We opened the manual to check it out. The pages revealed detailed information only the manufacturer could know—diagrams and descriptions that matched our car—and though we didn't test every single detail, we checked enough to become convinced this was the right book.

Cosmic Owner's Manual

The Bible claims to come from the Cosmic Manufacturer. So although its primary purpose is not to describe the physical details of the universe and Earth, what it says about them should match observable reality. Checking those details can be done more easily today than in the past because so many more characteristics of the universe, Earth, life, and humanity have been discovered—including the physics of our cosmic beginning. If authors writing 2,000 to 3,500 years ago accurately recorded detailed information about the universe, Earth, and life not found in any other ancient text, and if modern scientific discoveries consistently prove all that information correct, then we have powerful evidence those details must have been inspired by a Source beyond humanity.[1] Such demonstrated reliability also would give reasons to trust what the Bible says about *why* the universe is the way it is.

In every scientific discipline for which it has been tested, the Bible states something either unknown or contradictory to the beliefs at the time it was written. To document this research already has required several volumes, and many more are still to come.[2] For now, a brief overview of what the Bible says about nature's record shows how research findings confirm Scripture's capacity to accurately, consistently, and uniquely predict scientific discoveries centuries, even millennia, ahead.

The Bible Explains Where the Universe Came From

The authors of Scripture explicitly and repeatedly state that the universe had a beginning (see Gen. 1:1, 2:3–4; Ps. 148:5; Isa. 40:26, 42:5, 45:18; John 1:3; Col. 1:15–17; Heb. 11:3). This cosmic start was not relegated to the infinite past. The Bible declares it occurred in the finite past. Furthermore, this cosmic beginning was not just the start of the universe's matter and energy. It also marked the beginning of the space-time dimensions along which matter and energy are distributed.

Biblically speaking, time has not always existed (see "What Is Time?" p. 127). It began with the universe's creation. According to the Bible, the universe did not cause itself. Rather, a causal Agent operating from beyond or outside of matter, energy, space, and time created it.

The Hebrew phrase *hashamayim waw ha'erets* (translated "the heavens and the earth") refers to the entirety of the universe. It

---

What Is Time?

Time is difficult to define. Unlike space, accessible to humans in three dimensions, time is accessible to us in only one. And try as we might, we can neither stop nor reverse the arrow of time. What's more, it's impossible for any human to get outside the cosmic time dimension and observe all its properties.

Nevertheless, scientists, theologians, and philosophers have noted several immutable properties of time. Scholars agree that time is a dimension or realm in which cause-and-effect phenomena occur, with effects always following their causes. They also agree that apart from time, cause-and-effect phenomena anywhere in the universe cannot occur. In other words, time is integral to the operation of cause and effect.

Scientists observe a second property of time: a thermodynamic relationship. They measure the universe's total entropy (amount of disorder, or total amount of energy no longer available to perform work) as increasing in direct proportion to the passage of time. Time appears to be strongly linked with, or defined by, the second law of thermodynamics (the law of continuously increasing entropy or decay).

Psychologists, sociologists, philosophers, and theologians have also identified a relational property of time. They note that without time, relationships are impossible.[3] And what's more, the degree of depth, significance, and reward (or conflict) experienced in a relationship appears strongly correlated with the amount of time invested in it.

Scholars speculate about other properties of time as well, but not without considerable dispute. Only on these three time markers—the occurrence of cause and effect, the increase of entropy, and the development of personal relationships—has widespread agreement been achieved.

---

encompasses all matter, energy, space, and time. The Hebrew verb used for the universe's creation is *bārā'*, and given the context (Gen. 1:1), it indicates the making of that which did not previously exist.[4] Thus, Moses and other Old Testament prophets identified the Creator as the originator of matter, energy, space, and time.

The New Testament author of Hebrews wrote, "The universe was formed at God's command, so that what is seen was not made out of what was visible" (Heb. 11:3). The universe did not come from anything detectable. Researchers *can* detect matter, energy, and all the space-time dimensions associated with them. So the

Creator is said to have produced the detectable universe from that which cannot, by human means, be detected. Among all the "holy" books of the world's major religions, this idea in a coherent form is unique to the Bible.[5]

Because humans are trapped in time, where time is linear and cannot be halted or reversed, the idea that anything could exist "before" time defies imagination. Yet both the Old and New Testaments, uniquely among premodern texts, refer to God's activities "before the beginning of time" (see for example Prov. 8:22–23; John 1:1–3; 1 Cor. 2:7; and 2 Tim. 1:9).

From a scientific standpoint, the discovery that the universe had a beginning was a remarkable achievement.[6] More remarkable still, scientists now possess tools to explore various details of the cosmic beginning—detail sufficient to reveal the nature of that event. In studying these details, they are investigating what lies beyond the universe and whence the universe came.

Abundant observations verify that the universe started off infinitesimally small (see figure 9.1). Einstein's general relativity theory established relationships between matter and space-time and between energy and space-time. Therefore, if all the matter and energy in the universe once existed within an infinitesimal volume, it follows that all of space-time similarly was squished within an infinitesimal volume.

In 1970 British physicists Stephen Hawking and Roger Penrose published the first space-time theorem of general relativity.[7] Basing their work on only two major assumptions, Hawking and Penrose proved the cosmic beginning was not just the beginning of matter and energy but the beginning of space and time as well. In other words, space and time were created when the universe began.

The first of their two assumptions was and still is undisputed: the universe contains mass. The second assumption—that general relativity equations, to a high degree of reliability, describe the dynamics of massive bodies within the universe—at the time of the theorem's publication was still open to question.

Since then astronomers have applied ten or more independent tests of general relativity's reliability. The most definitive of those tests required close observation of binary neutron stars. Now that those observations have been completed, and on multiple neutron star binaries, general relativity is solidly confirmed—to better than a trillionth of a percent precision!

Roger Penrose says, "This [finding] makes Einstein's general relativity, in this particular sense, the most accurately tested theory known to science!"[8] Given the multiplicity of independent tests general relativity has passed, it also ranks as the most exhaustively and firmly established principle in all of physics. Thus all doubts about the creation of space and time would seem to have been removed.

Hawking and Penrose's theorem offered no guarantee, however, of applicability beyond the context of *classical* general relativity. So for the past few decades theoretical physicists worked to produce a whole family of space-time theorems. These additional theorems apply not only under the condition of classical general relativity but also in cosmic models where general relativity is augmented by quantum mechanics (quantum gravity big bang models) or by one or more scalar fields (inflationary hot big bang models). In the latter approach, the scalar fields are believed to generate a hyperfast and hyperbrief expansion episode when the universe is less than a quadrillionth of a quadrillionth of a second old. Even in all these possible scenarios, the space-time theorems apply. Space and time had a beginning.

While some theorists continue to propose models without a space-time beginning, these models invoke conditions that would not allow physical life to exist. For example, such models negate the second law of thermodynamics (which states there are preferred directions for physical processes, for example, from order to disorder and heat flows from hot sources to cold sources).

Theoretical physicists Arvind Borde, Alan Guth, and Alexander Vilenkin over a span of ten years published five more extensions of the space-time theorems.[9] These extensions established that all cosmological models, regardless of assumptions about homogeneity, isotropy or lack thereof, or energy conditions, must be subject to the relentless grip of an initial space-time singularity. Any reasonable cosmic model—that is, any model where the past obeys an averaged expansion condition (a necessary requirement for life to be possible)—must be traceable back within finite time to an actual beginning of space and time.

Given that space and time came into existence at the cosmic creation event, we can know something about where the universe came from. It must have arisen from a "realm" or "entity" beyond space and time.

Can we say that the universe was created out of nothing? The answer depends on the definition of nothing. When a son tells his mother there is nothing under his bed, he often means "nothing I want you to find out about." Similarly, scientists, theologians, and philosophers have different definitions of *nothing* depending on the context. It can mean a complete lack of:

1. matter;
2. matter and energy;
3. matter, energy, and the three big cosmic space dimensions (length, width, and height);
4. matter, energy, and all the cosmic space dimensions (including the six tiny space dimensions implied by string theories);
5. matter, energy, and all the cosmic space and time dimensions;
6. matter, energy, cosmic space and time dimensions, and created nonphysical entities;
7. matter, energy, cosmic space and time dimensions, created nonphysical entities, and other dimensions of space and time;
8. matter, energy, cosmic space and time dimensions, created nonphysical entities, and other dimensions or realms—spatial, temporal, or otherwise; or
9. anything and everything real, created or otherwise.

So what kind of nothingness did the universe come from? According to the space-time theorems of general relativity, not from the first five or possibly six kinds on this list. In other words, the universe could not possibly have arisen from matter, energy, and/or any of the space-time dimensions associated with them, either existing or previously existing. The reason number 6 remains open to debate is that, depending on one's theological/philosophical perspective, created nonphysical entities may or may not be endowed with the ability to create space-time dimensions.

The space-time theorems also eliminate option number 9. The universe of matter, energy, space, and time is, in itself, an effect. Every effect is generated by a cause. Absolute nothingness—the complete lack of anything and everything—cannot be a cause or causal agent. That is ruled out by definition and also by observation. If absolute nothingness could spontaneously produce something, scientists would see new somethings arising everywhere. Instead they see the consistent operation of the first law of thermodynamics, which says the total amount of matter and energy within the universe can neither be increased or decreased.

Astronomers' observations of the universe's past, tests of general relativity's reliability, and confirmations of the space-time theorems combine to establish that the universe was brought into existence by a causal Agent (see "Where Did the Cosmic Causal Agent Come From?" p. 132) with the capacity to operate before, beyond, unlimited by, and transcendent to all cosmic matter, energy, space, and time. In coming to these conclusions, the scientific community has confirmed, beyond reasonable doubt, this biblical description of the creation of the universe.

The Bible Explains the Universe's Features

Isaiah, Jeremiah, Job, Zechariah, and the psalmists declare that the universe is expanding and has continuously expanded from its beginning (see for example Job 9:8; Ps. 104:2; Isa. 40:22, 42:5, 44:24, 45:12, 48:13, 51:13; Jer. 10:12, 51:15; Zech. 12:1).[10] Jeremiah adds the important detail that the laws of physics are fixed (see Jer. 33:25). Several Old and New Testament passages also imply that laws governing the cosmos have not changed (see Gen. 1–3; Eccles. 1:4–11, 3:15; Rom. 8:18–23; Rev. 20:7–22:5). Paul, in the book of Romans, declares that the *entire* creation is subject to the law of decay (the second law of thermodynamics) (see Rom. 8:20–22).

Psalm 104:2 and Isaiah 40:22 describe the universe's continuous expansion as the "stretching out" of the heavens like a tent being unfurled. While all analogies are imperfect, this one seems to imply

Where Did the Cosmic Causal Agent Come From?

If God created the universe, who or what created God? Throughout the ages this theological question has been asked in a variety of ways.[11]

Some scientists raise it in an attempt to sidestep evidences for God. Oxford University biologist Richard Dawkins and University of Chicago evolutionary biologist Jerry Coyne argue that "if complex organisms demand an explanation, so does a complex designer."[12] Little children ask, "Who made God?" and philosophers ask, "How can there be an uncaused Cause?"

This question arises from personal experience with time, specifically from the manner in which time constrains us. For any being or entity restricted to a single time dimension, where time can neither be stopped nor reversed, every effect must be brought about by a previously existing cause. Everything restricted to the cosmic time line must be traceable back to a cause and a beginning.

The Cause responsible for bringing the universe into existence is not constrained by cosmic time. In creating our time dimension, that Agent demonstrated an existence above, or independent of, cosmic time.

Given that time is a dimension along which cause-and-effect phenomena can occur and because the cosmic causal Agent brought time into existence, that Agent at a minimum possesses the capacity to operate in the equivalent of two time dimensions. In this time "plane" (as opposed to time "line"), the cosmic causal Agent can choose to operate along a time line that's infinitely long and need not touch or cross the universe's time line. In the context of cosmic time, the causal Agent would have no beginning and no ending and would not be created.

Among the "holy" books of the world's religions, such a concept of the cosmic Cause is unique and original to the Bible.[13] Scripture refers to God as having no beginning or ending, as being uncreated (see Deut. 33:27; Job 36:26; Pss. 41:13, 90:2; Isa. 44:6; Dan. 4:34; John 1:1–3; Col. 1:15–17; Heb. 7:3, 24; Rev. 10:6). Psalm 90:4 and 2 Peter 3:8 say that God's time can be arbitrarily long or short compared to the human experience of time. Such complete freedom to compress or expand time is only possible for a Being who is completely free to operate beyond, or transcendent to, time (regardless of the number of time dimensions) or who has access to the equivalent of two or more time dimensions.[14] The Bible says God is both immanent (fully present) and transcendent with respect to time (see Gen. 1:1; Jer. 23:24; John 1:3; 1 Cor. 8:6; Col. 1:16–17; Heb. 11:3).

that just as the tent's surface expands as it is unfolded, so too the surface of the cosmos expands and spreads out.[15] Job 9:8 declares that God alone is responsible for the universe's stretching out. In light of this passage, human investigators of cosmic expansion should discover supernatural elements in its properties.

Not until the twentieth century did any other book—whether science, theology, or philosophy—even hint at the universe's continuous expansion. Today scientific advancements (see, for example, Figure 9.1, p. 134) have abundantly confirmed that it occurs and has occurred without interruption from the moment of creation onward, just as the Bible describes (see chapters 2 and 3, pp. 34–40, and 53–56).

Both observations and theory confirm a supernatural level of fine-tuning in the physical factors (dark energy density and mass density) governing the rate of cosmic stretching. That level exceeds by 10^{97} times the best example of human engineering design achievement.[16] The same observations and theory also establish that, like a tent, the universe's physical features reside in its surface. Lastly, measurements made at varying distances from Earth show that the laws of physics have remained constant throughout cosmic history to an extremely high degree.[17]

Biblical implications that the laws of physics have remained constant throughout cosmic history and that the entire universe is subject to those laws (the law of decay or second law of thermodynamics is mentioned in particular) dictate that the universe must get progressively colder as it gets older. Internal combustion engines illustrate the physical principle. When the engine's combustion chamber is compressed, the chamber's temperature rises. When the chamber expands, the temperature inside it drops. According to this law of decay, any physical system anywhere within the universe that expands under constant physical laws will experience a temperature drop proportional to the degree of expansion.

Virtually all the universe's heat energy is measurable within the cosmic background radiation, the radiation left over from the creation event. Figure 9.2 (p. 135) charts the temperature history of that radiation. Overlapping the measurements is the temperature-

Figure 9.1. Spreading Apart of Galaxies

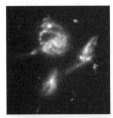

Images of distant galaxies compared with those nearby demonstrate the continuous expansion of the universe from an infinitesimal volume. The left image shows galaxies 11 to 12 billion light-years away when the universe was only 2 to 3 billion years old. The bottom illustration shows galaxies 2 billion light-years away when the universe was 12 billion years old. Galaxies in the left image are much farther apart than galaxies in the image below.

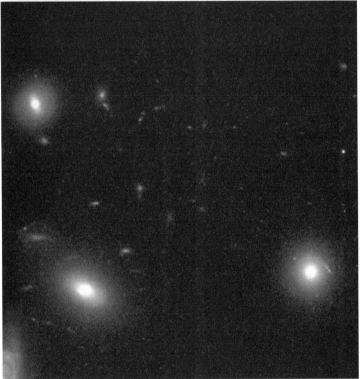

They are so close together that their mutual gravity rips away large segments of each galaxy into "tadpole" structures. Extrapolating the galaxies' spreading apart as the universe gets older back to the time of the universe's origin shows that the universe began infinitesimally small. (Image courtesy of NASA, N. Benitez [JHU], T. Broadhurst [Racah Institute of Physics/The Hebrew University], H. Ford [JHU], M. Clampin [STScI], G. Hartig [STScI], G. Illingworth [UCO/Lick Observatory], the ACS Science Team and ESA)

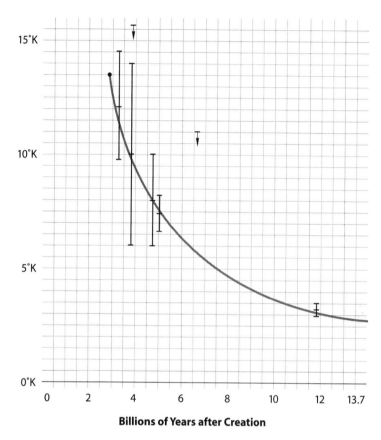

Figure 9.2. Cosmic Temperature Measurements Compared to Biblically Predicted Rate of Cosmic Cooling

This graph shows temperature measurements of the radiation left over from the cosmic creation event at eight different epochs spanning from the present to about 11 billion years ago,[18] back to when the universe was just one-fifth its present age. The overlapping curve shows the temperature drop from the creation event that would be expected if indeed the universe has expanded according to biblical constraints. (Illustration by Jonathan Price)

decline curve implied by the universe's age and by biblical statements about a cosmic beginning, continuous expansion from that beginning, and never-changing physical laws. The close fit of the data to the curve demonstrates the Bible's predictive power in describing cosmological details.

135

The Bible Explains Earth's Features

Scripture opens with these words: "In the beginning God created the heavens and the earth (the universe)" (Gen. 1:1). The focus of the passage shifts in the very next verse, which zeros in on Earth's surface and describes its initial conditions:

1. entirely covered with water
2. wrapped in darkness
3. devoid of life
4. unfit for life

Genesis 1:2 also records that under these hostile early conditions, the Spirit of God "hovered," or "brooded," over the waters. This Hebrew verb, *rā ap*, appears in only one other Old Testament passage. In Deuteronomy 32:11 it is used to describe God's giving birth and care to the Israelite nation as similar to a mother eagle's brooding over her hatchlings.

Job 38:8–9 explains the reason for the darkness on Earth's surface. An opaque cloud cover acted as a blanket, preventing any light from the Sun, Moon, and stars from reaching Earth's surface.

Recent scientific discoveries now affirm these biblical depictions of Earth's and life's early history. In the 1990s, planetary astronomers confirmed that Earth's primordial atmosphere was indeed initially opaque. Then, through an amazing set of circumstances, it changed. Research into the Moon's origin indicates that a Mars-sized planet collided with Earth at the just-right angle and speed to turn Earth's initial ocean into superheated steam, which blew away nearly all Earth's original atmosphere.[19] With the subsiding of asteroid and comet collision events over the next several hundred million years, Earth's atmosphere became translucent.[20] This outcome is consistent with the "let there be light" of the first creation day in Genesis 1:3.

Origin-of-life research now indicates a stunningly early date for life's origin, about 3.8 billion years ago, timing consistent with the biblical reference to an early start. Researchers also confirm that the origin of life occurred within a geologic instant without benefit of a primordial soup rich in prebiotic molecules.[21] This rapid beginning without a boost from previously existing molecular building blocks (amino acids, pentose sugars, nucleobases, or lipids) renders naturalistic origin-of-life scenarios unrealistic, leaving us to ponder a supernatural explanation.

The biblical implication (in Genesis 1:2) that Earth's first life was marine likewise fits the research data, which shows that the remains of Earth's first life are found exclusively in marine rocks.[22] So too does the biblical statement that just before life's origin on Earth, surface conditions were hostile.

Earth's early life helped establish a stable and abundant water cycle (see Gen. 1:6–8). Next came the buildup of landmasses. As shown in figure 3.5, "Growth of Continental Landmasses" (p. 52), continental landmass growth was particularly aggressive when Earth was slightly less than half its present age. Such a date is consistent with the Genesis narrative's placement of continental landmass growth as the first major occurrence of creation day three (see Gen. 1:9–10). All these initial events are described in the first ten verses of Genesis. On all counts, scientific investigation verifies the biblical details.

The Bible Explains Life and Its History

With light, rain, and land available, new life-forms began to take hold. Introduced and removed in a just-right sequence (see Ps. 104:27–30), those new life-forms paved the way for advanced life. They also contributed to dramatic changes in life's home: the transformation of Earth's atmosphere from permanently overcast to transparently clear, at least some of the time, and the pumping of enough oxygen into Earth's atmosphere to support large-bodied complex animal life (see Gen. 1:14–15).

With the Sun, Moon, and stars now visible to surface life, certain biological clocks could begin to regulate animal life, informing complex creatures when to feed, migrate, and reproduce. With these inner clock mechanisms in place and a large boost in the amount of atmospheric oxygen (see figure 3.4, p. 51), the stage was set for swarms of sea creatures (see Gen. 1:20) to burst upon the scene.

This part of the biblical creation story bears a remarkable resemblance to the scientific evidence for the Cambrian explosion.

That is the event some 543 million years ago when the number of Earth's animal phyla (a phylum designates life-forms sharing the same basic body plan) suddenly surged. Somewhere between 50 and 80 percent of all animal phyla ever to exist appeared in a geological instant.

The Bible Explains the Role of Advanced Animals

The Genesis 1 creation narrative, just one of about two dozen creation accounts in Scripture (see appendix D, "Creation Accounts in the Bible," p. 215), next mentions the creation of some new kinds of animals. The Hebrew language sets them apart from other animals with a word (*nepesh*) that refers to their "soulish" quality.[23] Their intelligence, emotional endowments, and capacity to relate to people make them unique. Many of these animals were domesticated for agricultural purposes and others tamed as pets. The creation accounts in Job suggest these creatures were designed by the Creator to serve and please the human race (see especially Job 39).

Anyone watching little children interact with animals can recognize the innate and powerful human desire to relate to certain creatures. Children seem to quickly learn the difference between soulish animals and non-soulish ones. Soulish animals have intellect, memory, a will of their own (in addition to instincts), innate motivations to nurture and protect, and a capacity to express feelings. While scientists have at least attempted to explain the origin of physical life from nonlife, no naturalistic explanation has yet been proffered for the origin of these soulish qualities of advanced animals. Rather, studies confirm that this soulishness sprang onto the biological scene suddenly and apparently out of nowhere.

The Bible's creation accounts stand alone among those of the world's religious texts and cultural traditions in recording a chronology for life's progression that perfectly matches the fossil record. With respect to advanced life, the text in Genesis 1:20–21 first mentions birds and sea mammals (generically) and then, without indication of when God created the first land mammals, goes on in Genesis 1:24–25 to introduce three specific kinds of land mammals:

"living creatures" or mammals that "move along the ground" (for example, rodents and hares), "wild animals" or mammals that are difficult to tame (for example, long-legged carnivores), and "livestock: or long-legged mammals that are easy to tame (for example, long-legged herbivores).[24] Last of all, the Bible describes the creation of humans.

Genesis 2:2 says that after creating the first humans, God rested, or ceased, from his physical creation work. For six epochs (see Appendix A, "Biblical Basis for an Ancient Universe and Earth," p. 207) God created. Then he stopped.

God's cessation from creation during the human era helps explain a perplexing enigma. The fossil record reveals a turnaround in speciation with the appearance of humans. Before humans, new species came on the scene at the rate of about one per year, on average. After humans appeared, the rate dropped to none per year. In natural habitats undisturbed by human activity, biologists have yet to observe the production of even one distinctly new (physiologically incapable of interbreeding) animal species.[25] Meanwhile, extinctions continue, even apart from human environmental abuse. The Bible offers an explanation for this puzzling feature of the fossil record: for six days God created; on the seventh day (the human era) he rests.

The Bible Explains What Makes People Different

According to the biblical story, the only earthly creatures God endowed with the capacity to communicate with him were humans. It says people not only share the birds' and mammals' soulish characteristics but also manifest some profound differences.

The Genesis text says God created the first human male and female "in his own image" (1:27). Volumes have been written on what this expression means. Among other things, it means every individual has a spiritual dimension—an awareness of a "self" and the capacity to imagine the thoughts and feelings of other individuals. And human soulish characteristics are developed to a far greater degree than those of any other creature.

People exhibit a curiosity beyond what basic survival, reproduction, and play require. It motivates questions such as "Who am

I?" "Why am I here?" "What makes the universe tick?" "Why is the universe the way it is?" "Is there a God?" "Why must people suffer?" and "What will happen to me when I die?"

This spiritual nature also causes individuals to devote significant time to reflection, meditation, and worship. And according to the creation accounts in Job and Psalms, just as God created advanced birds and mammals to serve and please humans, so he created people to serve and please him. This declaration of humanity's unique spiritual qualities leads to some specific scientific predictions. In particular, the introduction of humans to the chain of life should have resulted in a virtual explosion of culture. And that is exactly what anthropologists observe.

Humanity's arrival brought about the sudden and pervasive appearance of clothing, complex tools, jewelry, music, art, and religious ceremony.[26] Discounting technological advances, these cultural capabilities show no signs of evolving. The earliest humans were as expressive with their art, music, and spirituality as humans today.

Physical anthropologists have determined that only *Homo sapiens sapiens* (distinct from Neanderthals, *Homo erectus*, and archaic *Homo sapiens*) possess the brain structure to support various spiritual activities. Geneticists have demonstrated through mitochondrial DNA and Y-chromosomal DNA analysis that the present human species is traceable back to one man and one woman who lived less than 100,000 years ago. Many discoveries of the past decade have scientifically confirmed what the Bible says about the origin and nature of the human species.[27]

The Bible Reveals the Creator

Hundreds of Bible passages declare that the Cause of all things is a personal Being rather than a force or a principle. Only persons can create, plan, prepare, care, nurture, and act "on purpose." Forces and principles cannot.

What's more, persons communicate and relate at a level that is unique among all creatures. Genesis 2 describes how the first humans enjoyed rich and intimate conversation and interaction with God—until they rejected his authority and protection and struck out on their own. In that moment (described in Genesis 3), their early relationship with their Maker was profoundly and irreversibly, at least on their part, shattered. In their pride, humans thought they could make their own decisions about good and evil. They didn't need God to tell them. But when they recognized how wrong they were and what damage they had done, shame engulfed them and they ran away from his presence. Knowing God and relating to him became more challenging from that time on (see Gen. 3:8–10).

Given this breach and its far-reaching consequences, how could subsequent generations of humans come to know their Maker and enjoy perfect fellowship with him, as well as with each other? Given that he crafted the universe from that which cannot be detected, how can creatures locked within the universe come to know anything about him or what lies in that realm beyond?

No one could know the answers—as the creation accounts in Job, Psalms, Proverbs, and Romans point out—*unless* the Creator intended to make himself known by endowing creatures with the curiosity and capacity to investigate his clues. (For a list of major biblical creation passages, see appendix D, pp. 215–16.) These writings affirm that the Creator has given humanity two "books" to read and thereby discover not only the certainty of his existence but also essential truths about his character and purposes for humanity.

One book, of course, is the Bible. The other is the book of nature. One of the most famous Reformation creeds, the Belgic Confession of 1566, makes the point:

> We know him [God] by two means: First, by the creation, preservation, and government of the universe, since that universe is before our eyes like a beautiful book in which all creatures, great and small, are as letters to make us ponder the invisible things of God: his eternal power and his divinity, as the apostle Paul says in Romans 1:20.[28]

Through each generation's observational lens, including the sophisticated technologies and instruments of the current era, the universe reveals the cosmic causal Agent's characteristics. As the data are verified and compiled, his identity becomes increasingly clear. This God:

1. transcends the space-time dimensions of the universe;
2. planned and created the space-time dimensions of the universe;
3. is vastly more intelligent than the brightest human;
4. is vastly more knowledgeable than the best educated human;
5. is vastly more creative than the most imaginative human;
6. is vastly more powerful than the strongest human agency;
7. is consistent, reliable, and trustworthy;
8. is infinitely more caring and loving than the most devoted and nurturing human.

Only the God of the Bible both claims and manifests all these traits.

The Bible Describes a Realm beyond the Cosmos

Several passages of Scripture describe a realm where God and humans will dwell together—personally, freely, joyfully, and shamelessly—as soon as God completes the conquest and removal of all evil, death, and suffering. The scientific evidence and implications of this realm are the subjects of chapters 10–12. While such a place beyond the cosmos may seem out of reach, the Bible tells how humans can begin to access it even now.

The good news is that any believer in Jesus Christ, anywhere in the world, can communicate with God. Through that communication Jesus's followers can impact the life of any human being regardless of time, place, or circumstance. From a biblical perspective, prayer is the most powerful communication tool available to humans. It not only enhances our relationships with fellow humans but also allows us to build a close relationship with God himself.

Ironically, many people scoff at the idea that prayer is valuable—except perhaps as a comforting self-delusion. One reason is their rejection of God's conditions for the use of prayer, including humility and surrender to his authority. Another reason may be the widespread misconception that God must select whose prayers he listens and responds to because he couldn't possibly hear and respond to billions of people simultaneously.

The correction to this misconception is partly revealed in "Where Did the Cosmic Causal Agent Come From?" (p. 132). Because the Creator brought cosmic time into existence when he made the universe, he cannot be subject to or limited by humanity's time constraints. *For God, temporal experiences are not linear.* Because God caused cosmic time to come into effect and because one property of time is that it behaves as a dimension along which cause-and-effect phenomena occur, at minimum God must possess the capacity to freely operate in the equivalent of two or more time dimensions.

Given that God's communication link with humanity is at least two-dimensional with respect to time, then at any moment when billions of people are praying, he has the capacity to listen to each one along a time line that runs perpendicular to humanity's (see figure 9.3). A mere split second along humanity's time line could be indefinitely, even infinitely long on this perpendicular time line.

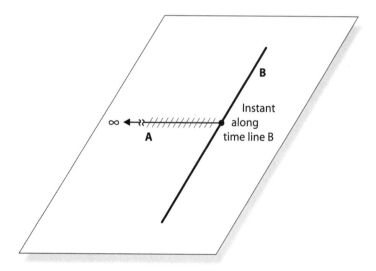

Figure 9.3. Listening to Billions of Simultaneous Prayers

One of many possible ways God could give individual attention to several billion prayers all uttered at the same moment would be to listen to those prayers along a time line perpendicular to the universe's. Along this type of time line, a microsecond could stretch into trillions of years or even longer.

Thus, God would have no problem giving individual attention and response to six billion prayers that all arrive at the same moment in human, or cosmic, time. Furthermore, as the Creator of any and all existing time dimensions (or their equivalent), God is unconfined by time and has many possible ways to listen and respond to billions of simultaneous prayers.

Because God in his temporal capacities transcends the human time dimension, he is never stressed or wearied by relationships. Humans, on the other hand, constrained as we are by the dimensions and physics of the universe (for the reasons why, see chapter 11), constantly feel that limitation. We possess a strong desire to spend more quality time with loved ones and the Creator himself. But time and energy do not allow unlimited interaction, and painful decisions on who to shortchange must always be made. God never lacks for "time" and never shortchanges anyone who comes to him.

A Trustworthy Testament

Many theologians express concern over treating, or rather mistreating, the Bible as a science textbook. They quote Galileo in warning readers that the Bible's primary purpose is to tell us how to go to heaven, not how the heavens go.[29] While the Bible certainly focuses on revealing God's plan for eternity, nevertheless, the information it includes about the origin, history, and operation of the universe is abundant and impressive.

What makes the Bible's claims about the origin, structure, and history of the universe and life all the more remarkable is that it stood alone for so long in making such claims. For centuries the Bible was the only text offering such precise and voluminous detail about the natural realm.

The detailed predictive accuracy of the Bible's authors in addressing all these topics supplies confirming evidence that the God of the Bible created the universe and wrote the instruction manual for humanity's specific benefit. The accuracy of biblical predictions reassures us that the Bible can be trusted in what it says about every issue—scientific and nonscientific. We have sound reasons to trust

Scripture's insights on why the universe, as wonderfully designed as it is for humankind's specific benefit, nonetheless has features that make this life less than idyllic, sometimes even uncomfortable.

These insights allow us to address this crucial and frequently asked question: If God really did create the universe for humanity's benefit, why does it contain so many features that involve pain, suffering, and death? Given his proven power and his apparent care for the human species, couldn't God have made a better place to live? If there is such a thing as "paradise," why don't we have a perfect universe now? The next chapter addresses these challenging questions.

10

Why Not a Perfect Universe—Now?

Dwindling petroleum reserves have many people scrambling to find alternative fuels. Alison, a friend and RTB volunteer with a background in both science and medicine, has found ways to process a variety of fat waste products into fuel for her biodiesel Volkswagen. Whether leftovers from the deep fryer vats of fast food restaurants or household cooking grease, these resources can power her car. But with the growing number of biodiesel vehicles in the Los Angeles area, Alison is finding it more difficult to obtain adequate waste-fat fuel. She's currently researching new sources—and better alternatives.

Strangely, we often believe something better is possible even when it can't yet be produced. In some cases it can't even be identified. Though experience frequently reminds us that "good" is the best we can achieve, perfection is what we really want.

So what does perfection look like? To define the word requires a context.

Astronomers' observations show that in the context of the laws of physics, the Earth, Moon, solar system, Milky Way Galaxy, and Local Group—indeed the entire universe—are all perfectly designed to provide a wonderful, bountiful home for humanity (see chapters 2–8). Yet no one, including astronomers, would claim that life on Earth is perfect.

Most people define the perfect home for humanity as a place where "bad stuff" doesn't happen. As diverse as the world's cultures may be, people everywhere mostly agree on what to get rid of to make the world a better place—injustice, oppression, deprivation, disease, and physical, mental, and emotional injuries/impairments. The list could go on, but even this brief summary supplies a context for the "perfect paradise" people long for. It's a place where fairness, freedom, and fullness are the norm for every individual. A place without fear, stress, or anxiety. A place free of injury, disease, suffering, and disability. In other words, the perfect place is like the Garden of Eden, only on a global scale.

That is exactly the type of paradise God gave the first humans. He started them off in a pristine garden and instructed them to manage and expand it. Yet our world is nothing like Eden. It is full of evil and suffering, which cause countless people to question God's existence and their purpose for living. Couldn't God have come up with a better plan?

The Bible says he instructed the first humans to "be fruitful and increase in number; and fill the earth" (Gen. 1:28), to manage Earth's resources wisely for the benefit of all life. God certainly gave the first humans plenty to work with.

A Lavish Domain

Not only astronomers but philosophers and theologians too stand in awe of the magnificence of all that has been made for humanity's benefit. Some three thousand years ago, Israel's King David marveled,

> We are filled with the good things of your house. . . . You care for the land and water it; you enrich it abundantly. The streams of God are filled with water to provide the people with grain. . . . You crown the year with your bounty, and your carts overflow with abundance.
>
> Psalm 65:4, 9, 11

When researchers focus on Earth's surface, they observe an abundance of provision for humankind along with an extravagance of beauty and elegance. The apostles Paul and Barnabas reminded Lystra's citizens nearly two thousand years ago, God "has not left himself without testimony: He has shown kindness by giving you rain from heaven and crops in their seasons; he provides you with plenty of food and fills your hearts with joy" (Acts 14:17).

Today, with a human population topping six billion, Earth still offers plentiful supplies. In fact, the universe and Earth seem lavishly over-endowed for humanity's survival. There is enough here for people to enjoy a magnificent environment, eat delightful food, spend quality time with others, access technology, and experience pleasure of all kinds—spiritual, intellectual, emotional, and physical. We easily could get by with less. Unfortunately, most people do, and many starve, but not because of undersupply.

Along with the Creator's obvious extravagance toward humanity come equally obvious examples of chaos, greed, oppression, evil, and suffering of many kinds. Who can help but wonder what happened? Where's paradise? Where is our perfect world?

The evidence from nature and the Bible's message offer a consistent answer. The Creator cares for humanity more than we can imagine. He is all-powerful, unlimited by any cosmic constraints. The conditions of the universe and the Earth are perfect for fulfillment of his current purposes for humanity. Once again the word *perfect* requires a context.

Perfectly Prepared

Many scientists would say the universe is the way it is because there is only one way to build a cosmos that supports intelligent physical life.[1] According to this perspective the pain, suffering, and death experienced by humanity and all life arises from the fact that only one set of physical laws and only one kind of universe permit the existence of life and humans. On this basis some claim the Creator had only one way to build humanity's home.

Hundreds of features of the universe appear to support this conclusion. The Milky Way Galaxy, solar system, and physical laws must be exquisitely fine-tuned to make human life possible.[2] As preceding chapters explain, if any one of these features were changed even a little, people could not exist at any time or place in the universe.

This fine-tuning, however, serves the needs of physical life as we know it, life confined to a particular set of space-time dimensions. Different kinds of physical or nonphysical life within a different dimensional system, such as one that involves super-dimensions or permits more than the familiar spatial and temporal capacities, would arise from a completely different set of fine-tuned characteristics. If the Creator were to make appropriate adjustments to the physical nature of humans, he would have many options for their housing.

The idea that God has options in designing humanity's abode is explicitly stated in the Bible. The last two chapters of Revelation describe a "new creation" completely different from this present universe. Whereas other religions promise a restoration of paradise such as the one humans initially enjoyed in Eden, the Bible offers humanity complete deliverance from an imperfect paradise into a purely perfect realm.

From a biblical perspective, Eden (paradise) was gloriously beautiful and bountiful. Nevertheless, the laws of physics and dimensions of length, width, height, and time operated there— even before Adam and Eve's rebellion. These laws and dimensions shackled humans, to some degree, right from the start (see chapter 11, pp. 167–77 and chapter 13, pp. 195–203).

The universe's physical laws and dimensions not only limited the ability of humans to relate to one another, to other creatures (both terrestrial and angelic), and to God, but they also guaranteed that all physical life would decay and die. Adam and Eve were the only exceptions, *if* they would eat from the Tree of Life (Gen. 2:9, 3:22). These laws and dimensions did not change when Adam and Eve chose instead to eat from a different tree, disregarding both the Creator's gift and the Creator's authority (Gen. 2:16–17; 3:2–7). Their choice, freely made, came as no surprise to God despite the pain it brought. From the moment spiritual death (autonomy from God) invaded creation, physical death became a blessing, an avenue through which God could temper the outbreak of evil and suffering.

More importantly, through death—his own and that of human beings—the Creator could enact his plan of redemption. That's why God, after humanity's rebellion, barred access to the Tree of Life (see Gen. 3:22). The fruit of this tree would have kept the now sin-marred humans from experiencing physical decay and the consequences of injury and disease—tools God would use to restrain sin's expression (see chapters 11 and 12). But God's love did not allow this tragedy.

This universe with all its features, laws, and dimensions represents the perfect theater for enactment of God's redemptive drama (see chapter 11, pp. 177–79). By its physical constraints, God limits the spread of evil, encourages the pursuit of virtue, and demonstrates his great love for humankind. According to the Bible, this temporal universe provides an essential proving ground to test each human heart (in the spiritual sense) and prepare those who pass the test for life in a completely new realm, one that includes all the features we long for and more—the perfection we can barely imagine (see "The New Creation—Better Than Paradise" and chapter 13).

The New Creation—Better Than Paradise

Radically different from the Garden of Eden (paradise), this new realm has no thermodynamics, gravity, or electromagnetism.[3] It has no darkness despite the lack of sun and stars.[4] It's temporality is not confined to a single dimension.[5] The new creation is so magnificent, pleasurable, and rewarding that no earthly human can fully visualize its wonders (see 1 Cor. 2:9). (For a more detailed description of the new creation's features, see chapter 13.)

In this new domain, there is no death, pain, sickness, suffering, crying, or grief (see Rev. 21:3–5; 22:1–5). Thus, from a biblical perspective, the new creation reflects the fact that God indeed is loving, caring, and powerful enough to create for humans a home completely free of anything even momentarily harmful or unpleasant. So there must be excellent reasons why this present universe—as wonderful, beautiful, and bountiful as it is—brings about pain, suffering, and death for all life, including humans (see chapters 11 and 12).

False Assumptions

Skeptics who complain that an all-loving, all-powerful, all-wise God would have done a much better job of creation make a faulty assumption—that such a God never would have allowed evil to touch his creation at any time or place. Such a God, they say, would have made the universe permanently free from pain, trouble, death, and evil.

Nothing seems to perplex humanity as much as the subject of evil. Some say the existence of evil is a paradox wrapped in an enigma enshrouded in mystery embedded in riddle implanted in a puzzle inside a giant maze. As complex as the question of evil may be, however, the human mind relentlessly pursues answers. Greater intellects than mine have tackled the problem of evil without unraveling all its intricacies. Yet my formal training in physics and mathematics, combined with an extensive study of theology and the Bible, has given me, by God's grace, a few insights worth considering.

First, the assumption that an all-loving, all-powerful God would never permit evil refutes itself. The concept of evil cannot arise in a "neutral" universe, one without a divine Maker. The skeptic presumes to judge God by a standard that does not exist apart from God. How could anyone "judge" any behavior if human beings were merely the mindless, spontaneous, temporary outcome of purposeless and undirected physical processes?

Second, that assumption gains emotional force from the implication that evil and suffering are inescapable components of the one and only permanent reality. But what if they are temporary? Suppose they are part of a realm that does not, when it ends, mean the end of human life. Then might they serve a purpose? In an eternal scheme of things, could humanity's current experience of evil and suffering possibly be likened to a semester's worth of trial and toil for a student who undergoes preparation for a worthwhile career? In that case suffering and encounters with evil may possibly carry some significance and value.

If science and philosophy are correct in claiming that effects can't exceed their causes, then the human mind, which cannot be explained by nature alone,[6] must come from the Creator. That mind persistently whispers of a reality beyond the limits that currently bind us—limits imposed by space, time, matter, energy, and the laws by which they interact.

Misperceptions

Unfortunately, we try to define this creation according to our limited human understanding. In the process, many people cling to two suppositions that intensify the problem of evil instead of explaining it.

Misperception #1: God created the universe only to provide a comfortable environment for life and humans. Examining Eden in a broader context reveals that it was not the ultimate paradise many people presume. Even before Adam and Eve's rebellion ushered in sin's effects, the Garden required maintenance. The first human beings had to work the land and tend its plants (see Gen. 2:15). Eden's creatures needed to eat, sleep, and be cared for too.

As part of Earth's surface, the Garden would be subject to the storms, earthquakes, floods, and fires sometimes referred to as "natural evils." These forces play crucial roles in distributing and replenishing essential nutrients for life, but often they also damage and destroy. In addition, the same anatomical systems that permitted Adam and Eve the pleasures of taste and touch also provided the experience of pain—which brings anguish but also serves to protect.

Eden's greatest "danger" lay in human free will. And yet eliminating it would negate the worth of what most essentially distinguishes us from other creatures. Genesis 1 declares that humans are created in the "image" of God (vv. 26–27). Most theologians agree that part of this image is the capacity to exercise choice in priorities, values, and relationships. This wide-ranging capacity to choose enables humans to experience deep fulfillment. Free choice leads to expressions of virtue, justice, mercy, and love—the very things that give life meaning.

Misperception #2: Nothing exists beyond the universe. A place where we can exercise free will presents the perfect context to test our allegiance. Human destiny begins here in the first creation, but it does not end with it any more than driving stops the day one passes the licensing exam. This drama began even before humanity entered the scene, in a realm outside the cosmic space-time dimensions. There the most beautiful and powerful being among the spiritual creatures, namely angels (see Ezek. 28:12–19),[7] promoted himself as God's equal (see Isa. 14:13–14). According to Scripture, a third of Lucifer's peers followed him in rebellion (see Rev. 12:1–9). They chose irreversible enmity with God.

But God chose to make other spiritual creatures—humans—along with a host of other living things. Why he did, we can barely begin to comprehend. Clearly this creation is an expression of his divine nature, and there is likely much more to the explanation. For now, though, the most important fact is that God *did* create—on purpose.

Perfection Defined by Purpose

God made the universe the way he did not just for one purpose but for many.

Purpose #1: The Creator Wanted Humans to Exist

The Creator obviously wanted humans to exist. But he had greater plans for humanity than mere existence. Thus, he optimized cosmic circumstances to accomplish those specific plans—most importantly, to prepare us for life face-to-face with him, forever, fully free and without risk of ruin. The Bible's pages bring that preparation process with its multiple facets into focus.[8] An initial glimpse at the two-creation scenario provides a context for understanding humanity's story in relation to God's ultimate intent. A careful study of that story reveals multiple additional purposes behind God's creation of a seemingly "imperfect" universe.

Purpose #2: God Made This Universe to Serve as a Classroom for Humans

God could have designed the universe to provide a home for humans exclusively, but apparently he did not want us to be alone without physical companions. Instead, he created the universe in such a way as to support an astonishing array of diverse life-forms, many of which share the planet with us still.

These creatures all make their own special contribution to humanity's support and well-being. Not only do they benefit us physically, but their behavior teaches us valuable life lessons. In a debate with his philosopher friends, Job exhorted them, "But ask the animals, and they will teach you, or the birds of the air, and they will tell you; or speak to the earth, and it will teach you, or let the fish of the sea inform you" (Job 12:7–8).

Job introduced this creation theme—one developed throughout all the Bible's poetic books (Job, Psalms, Proverbs, Ecclesiastes, and Song of Solomon). Every life-form on Earth can instruct human beings in some specific and useful way. Solomon advised us to look to the ants to learn about industriousness (see Prov. 6:6). Other creatures provide exquisite examples of the character traits universally valued and worthy of emulation—loyalty, courage, resourcefulness, devotion, orderliness, responsibility, teamwork, focus, initiative, and more.

Lessons can be profound even at the smallest end of life's spectrum, now visible thanks to technological advances. The smallest entity truly alive (able to survive on its own) is the cell. Inside the cell are certain molecules—proteins, DNA, and RNA. These molecules bear an uncanny resemblance to the machines, computers, and interfaces humans build and use. The basic designs are comparable, as are the functions they perform. The one significant difference is that life molecules operate with far greater efficiency and reliability than their human analogues. We have much to learn from them.

The molecules of life are organized into the equivalent of factories. These factories are organized into the equivalent of cities replete with transportation systems, resource distribution, waste management, repair sites, and command and control centers. Again, the only significant difference between the factories and cities in the cell and their human analogues is the cell's greater efficiency and reliability.

These tiny life molecules help demonstrate what it means to be created in the "image of God." Long before knowing such molecules existed, human beings created using the same basic designs. Living cells also reveal that humans are not equivalent to God. Our design capabilities and achievements rank far below what can be seen inside the simplest and the smallest of his creatures. (Biochemist Fazale Rana, a colleague of mine, has devoted an entire book to this theme.[9]) Intellectual capacity is not the only limiting factor, however. Moral/ethical weaknesses hinder human enterprise and achievement all the more.

Purpose #3: God Made This Universe to Demonstrate His Divine Nature

From the most ancient writings yet unearthed, we learn that the earliest humans responded to the heavens just as people today do—with awe and wonder, recognizing a power beyond any earthly source (see for example Psalm 8). Our awareness of the power required to make and sustain virtually any aspect of the cosmos continues to increase with time and discovery. Yet the Creator's power is just one characteristic that can be seen in what he has made and in the way he made it.

Study of the universe reveals more than just the Creator's attributes of power, intelligence, knowledge, creativity, consistency, reliability, trustworthiness, care, and love. Research shows something of the extent to which he manifests each of these qualities—far beyond mere human potential. Every detail of creation reveals a Creator who, though transcendent to and unlimited by space, time, matter, and energy, attended to the minute particulars of his handiwork.

The world of nature—on whatever scale it is examined—reads like a book revealing God's worthiness to receive worship in all the languages of humankind. On those occasions when God communicated in words, his message came with clarity and testability rather than with vagueness or riddles. He purposed to make himself known in both his books—the book of nature and the Bible.

Purpose #4: God Made This Universe to Show Us Our Own Human Nature

In addition to introducing us to God and his attributes, the universe introduces us to ourselves. It reveals both the wonders and the horrors of human nature. Here again, God's design of the universe and Earth to support a wide diversity of birds and mammals reflects purpose and planning, for these creatures make excellent mirrors. Because they are endowed with intelligence, will, and the capacity to express and respond to emotions, they bond with human beings in unique ways. According to Scripture (see Job 39) and field observations, these advanced animals, each species in its own way, are innately motivated to serve and to please humans. This motivation seems evident in the birds and mammals we relate to as pets. But it also shows up in those that have lacked human contact and thus have never experienced human abuse.

I observed this motivation firsthand during solo hikes in some remote parts of the Canadian Rockies and Selkirk Mountains. Birds and mammals there showed no fear of me. In fact, after taking a few moments to observe me, they seemed eager to approach and make contact. At the time I couldn't help but think about the harmony Adam and Eve initially enjoyed in Eden. Nor could I help but ponder the different response of creatures that encounter humans more frequently. Sadly, their instinct tells them to run, fly, or hide.

My Canadian wildlife encounters brought another theological insight. If birds and mammals are endowed by the Creator with a powerful desire to serve and please human beings, then perhaps we too have been endowed with an innate desire for relationship with a higher Being.

Personal observation over the past few decades tells me that the greatest earthly fulfillment humans experience comes from serving and pleasing God. This observation finds confirmation in countless stories from all parts of the globe. The first question of the Westminster Shorter Catechism reads, "What is the chief end of man?" The Catechism's answer: "Man's chief end is to glorify God, and to enjoy him forever."[10] God graciously linked the pursuit of our chief purpose with our greatest experience of joy.

Unfortunately, the capacity for sin and evil within humans has derailed our relationships both with God and our fellow creatures. That capacity found expression in the first human decision to go against the Creator's authority. Since then, humans' sin-warped behavior tends to drive birds and mammals away. It also causes us to run from God, to argue that he doesn't really exist, or to pretend that Adam and Eve's rebellion never happened or was no big deal if it did.

Yet throughout our environment, we see the devastation sin and evil have caused. The productivity and beauty of the land, sea, and air have been diminished. Earth's plants are no longer as productive and nutritious as they once were. Thousands of animal species have vanished. Ironically, the extinction damage has been greatest among those species (birds and mammals) that serve and please us best.[11]

As Paul explains in Romans, "the whole creation has been groaning as in the pains of childbirth right up to the present time" (8:22). (For more on the meaning of this passage, see chapter 11, pp. 168–69.) Humanity's treatment of Earth and of its creatures exposes our penchant for selfishness, greed, and foolishness, not to mention our arrogance (see Isa. 59:2–15). In other words, God designed the universe to house an array of special creatures through which he could show us our uniqueness and capacity for magnificence as well as the depth of our depravity and our desperate need for him.

Purpose #5: God Made This Universe to Provide for Rapid Development of Global Civilization and Technology

God commanded the first humans to "be fruitful and increase in number; fill the earth and subdue it" (Gen. 1:28).[12] In the New Testament Jesus gave his followers the additional directive to "go and make disciples of all nations [people groups]" (Matt. 28:19).

Effective oversight of all Earth's resources for the benefit of all life and for effective worldwide communication of what it means to be Christ's disciples requires a fairly high level of globally distributed technology. Therefore, one of God's purposes for making the universe the way it is, including the physical laws and timing and layering of life on Earth, was to supply the necessary resources for completion of these assignments.

Purpose #6: God Made This Universe to Display His Glory and Goodness

The universe appears to be supernaturally crafted for observation, and humanity happens to be supernaturally positioned for the best possible view. Technology has allowed researchers not only to observe but also measure the universe—its age, extent, content, and hundreds of other features (see chapters 2–6, pp. 30–40, 44–56, 59–76, 80–92, and 96–106). As these observations and measurements accumulate, humans continue to discover more of God's glory, power, creativity, goodness, and love.

Purpose #7: God Made This Universe for the Conquest of Evil

As an expression of his love for humanity, God created the universe the way he did to protect us from a future touched by evil. He made this cosmos to serve as an arena in which evil and suffering can be rooted out, finally and eternally—while simultaneously maintaining the human capacity to exercise free will and, thus, to experience and express love.

His cosmic design facilitates this conquest as quickly and painlessly as possible, not for him but for his creatures (see "Rapid Conquest and Removal of Evil," p. 160). This idea that God designed the universe's physics and dimensions for the purpose of bringing about the ultimate conquest and removal of evil (and the suffering it causes) is more fully developed in chapter 11.

Purpose #8: God Made This Universe for the Instruction of His Angels

Humans take center stage in the unfolding drama of God's ultimate victory over evil. We directly experience something from God the Bible calls "grace," from a Greek word defined as "unmerited favor," in a way God's angels cannot easily comprehend.

Humans have the opportunity to choose metamorphosis from spiritual death (a state of spiritual autonomy) to spiritual life (submission to God's authority). We can exchange the condemnation incurred by our moral imperfection for God's forgiveness and redemption. Individuals can escape eternal separation from God as

---

Rapid Conquest and Removal of Evil

Many skeptics and believers in God complain that 13.73 billion years seems like a long time for God to spend accomplishing his purposes for the universe. "Couldn't an all-powerful, all-loving God bring us the new creation's benefits in something less than several billion years?"

Chapter 3, page 44–56 explains why the universe takes 13.73 billion years (at a minimum) to mature sufficiently for the support of human life. Recent measurements by anthropologists and geneticists indicate that humans came on the cosmic scene as late as 100,000 years ago or less.[13] According to both physics and the Bible, the human era will likely continue no more than a few thousand or tens of thousands of years.[14] So the total time of humanity's exposure to evil seems incredibly brief, in astronomical terms. Each individual's exposure is briefer still. It is a testimony to God's mercy that he carefully nurtures the universe for 13.73 billion years and yet limits our time within its boundaries to a mere split second on the cosmic clock.

---

they embrace eternal life and fellowship with God. We can trade our best efforts and worst deeds for growth in the character traits of our Creator and Rescuer, Jesus Christ.

Angels are different. Those who remained obedient to God and did not succumb to evil must learn about grace and the "manifold wisdom of God" (Eph. 3:10) by observing them at work in humans (see Eph. 3:8–11; 1 Cor. 4:9; 1 Peter 1:12). That angels are highly motivated to learn about God's love and grace is made clear in the writings of Luke, Paul, Peter, and the author of Hebrews (see Luke 15:10; 1 Cor. 4:9; 6:3; 11:10; Heb. 1:14; 13:2; 1 Peter 1:12). These men describe angels as intently watching humans to discover insights about divine grace (see 1 Cor. 4:9). Apparently one purpose for the universe's design is to give angels a clear view and deeper understanding of the God they serve, of his grace, and of his plans for the future.

Purpose # 9: God Made This Universe to Personally Initiate Our Rescue

Personal sacrifice defines heroes. It shows character as nothing else can. Most of all, it shows love.

Personal sacrifice beyond comprehension brought the Creator to accept the confines of earthly life in a human body in the midst of human nature. He willingly accepted all the hardships and humiliations associated with life among his sin-marred creatures. No one has ever been more misunderstood than he.

As the only sinless being, he suffered the full penalty justice demands for all humanity's sin against God and wrongdoing to others. Every evil thought, word, attitude, and action sin has produced or will ever produce was paid for by Christ's sacrifice on the cross (see 1 John 1:7–10, 5:11–12; Matt. 5:16–22, 27–28).

Because the Creator himself, innocent and capable as he was, chose to suffer and pay the full penalty for all of humanity's rebellion against God, a means was made available for individuals to receive forgiveness and redemption from all the darkness within themselves. This plan to rescue us required a universe with characteristics that would make possible the Creator's physical presence on the terrestrial scene. People needed to witness Christ the Creator's character, hear his teaching, and observe his actions on their behalf firsthand.

Purpose #10: God Made This Universe to Amaze Us with His Grace

Some people give up hope and surrender to despair or evil when they realize they can't achieve genuine goodness. Others convince themselves that because no one is perfect, being "better" than at least some other people makes them good enough. Many people vacillate between these two extremes, alternately nagged by an inner voice reminding them that they fall short and consoled by the rationalization that everyone does. But to every human, God makes the same astonishing offer.

We can enter his presence based on Jesus Christ's perfect and complete sacrifice rather than on our own best (or worst) efforts. He is our hope, our only hope, and he purposely designed the universe so anyone who is willing can perceive and receive these truths.

We can live beyond the cosmos with him in his splendor or live beyond the cosmos without him, apart from all he is. Not only does

Jesus make this offer, but he also provides people with the faith to receive it. That faith is available as a free gift.

Purpose #11: God Made This Universe to Prepare and Train Us for What Lies Ahead

Far from what popular culture depicts as "heaven," the realm beyond the universe is not a realm of pure or boring leisure. Rather, the new creation is a place where God's people will be engaged in the most challenging work of their lives.

While the Bible does not give our complete job description, it does offer a summary. Those who choose to spend eternity with God will rule with him over all that comprises the new creation. Specifically, we will serve in roles roughly comparable, in earthly terms, to kings, priests, judges, teachers, and magistrates over the angels and over whatever or whomever God creates and designs for his new realm (see 1 Cor. 6:2–3; 1 Peter 2:9; Rev. 20:6).

This future work requires education and training. God designed this universe to equip human beings for full participation in and appreciation of the coming creation.

The current assignment to carry God's message of love, life, and truth (see 1 John 1:5, 2:17–24, 3:16–24, 4:2–12, 16–19) to the ends of the Earth and to teach people from all ethnic groups what it means to be followers of Christ (see Matt. 28:18–20)—with gentleness, respect, and a clear conscience (see 1 Peter 3:15–16)—demands growing maturity fueled by God's Spirit. The Spirit is a source without limit to empower people to keep moving in the right direction. With that growing maturity comes an increasing capacity to carry out our God-given assignments in the new creation. That growth also brings an increasing capacity to enjoy the rewards that lie ahead.

Triumph of Good over Evil

God made the universe the way it is to help accomplish as efficiently as possible the ultimate and eternal triumph of good over evil. He so designed the universe that his victory could be achieved for humanity's specific and enduring benefit, rather than for our annihilation. The apostles Peter and Paul say that even angels long to see and understand how God uses the universe, in part, as a vehicle to rescue fallen human creatures from themselves and prepare them for life in his presence where there will no longer be any risk of future rebellion (see 1 Cor. 4:9; Eph. 3:10; 1 Peter 1:12).

It's astounding that a single universe could simultaneously accomplish such a complexity of intertwined yet distinct purposes. Skeptics who claim God could have made a better home for humanity might ponder what it would take to design a home that simultaneously accomplishes all this one does. Furthermore, if we are humble we may recognize that the Creator may have other purposes for the universe that he has not yet chosen to reveal to us. We can expect at least some mysteries to remain regarding why the universe is the way it is.

For certain, this universe is not perfect in an ultimate sense. But it is perfect *for now*. How God uses the physics and dimensions of this universe to bring about his victory over evil and prepare his followers for rewards and service in the new creation is the subject of the next chapter.

11

Why These Physical Laws and Dimensions?

When I joined Caltech's radio astronomy research team, it never occurred to me that the lack of a driver's license would be a problem. My plan for transportation involved my two legs, a bicycle, and for longer trips, buses, trains, and planes—same as I'd used in Canada. However, when I signed up for my first observing run at the Owens Valley Radio Observatory some 250 miles north of campus, I found out my plan wouldn't work. People laughed when I inquired about buses and trains. A car was the only way to get there.

So I needed a driver's license, and I needed it fast. In addition, I needed effective training so I wouldn't damage the car pool vehicles. Fortunately, one driver's education school could fit me into their intensive program. They guaranteed rapid results if I gave the right amount of time and effort to their training. Within two weeks I had my license, and not once did I ever scratch or dent one of Caltech's cars.

The new creation is somewhat like that observatory: there's only one way to get there (and it's discussed later in this chapter). But, much like the driver's school I attended, intensive training in this creation can prepare us for eternity in the next realm.

The efficiency and effectiveness of that training arises in part from the manner in which the Creator defined our classroom—with exquisitely designed physical laws and space-time dimensions. The instruction and preparation they offer become increasingly effective according to the priority given them.

God's Training Program

Many people wonder why an all-loving, all-powerful Creator would subject humans to the tribulations and tragedies of this world. One partial answer may be that if evil and suffering are temporary and humans eternal, then each person's encounters with these troubles and griefs may serve as preparation for some high reward not possible otherwise. This consideration might also imply that humans are part of God's strategy to bring about a total and permanent triumph of good over evil.

The idea that our present exposure to evil and suffering may have some higher purpose finds additional support in the uniqueness of human morality and evil. Humanity's acknowledgment of and striving for goodness in the moral/ethical sense is not expressed in any other species. Nor is there any evidence that these characteristics naturally evolved. Artifacts and records from the most ancient civilizations indicate that people living ages ago showed the same level of concern for morality and ethics as do people today.

Humanity's capacity to commit evil also is unique. No other species, past or present, shares it. Likewise, the human propensity for evil did not gradually evolve over tens of thousands of years. Anthropological and archeological studies confirm that this capacity emerged as suddenly as humans appeared.

This unprecedented concern about morality and ethics in the first humans, along with their capacity and inclination to commit evil, implies that such traits were not accidents of nature. Rather, they must have been purposely instilled for important reasons.

As noted in chapter 7 (pp. 108–18), scientific evidence provides a reasonable basis for humanity's hope that the experiences of life, good and bad, mean something and lead somewhere. The laws of physics and their impact on behavior suggest that our training has present and future purposes that relate to the paradox of evil as well as prepare individuals for life in the new creation.

Laws of Physics and Behavior Modification

Some of the ways physical laws mold and direct human behavior seem more obvious than others. Infants struggle against the law of gravity but quickly learn to avoid its consequences by submitting to its rules. As babies mature into toddlers, then into teens, and then into young adults, they discover how much work must be expended and wisely channeled to keep the second law of thermodynamics at bay. What we call "Murphy's Law" implies that things get messier or more chaotic all by themselves, but experience indicates that certain human behaviors greatly multiply the effect. For example, the teenager who can't be bothered to apply sunscreen may find as an adult that excess exposure to electromagnetic radiation increases skin cancer risk and leads to premature aging. Then the effort seems worthwhile.

Behavior modifications induced by the manner in which the laws of physics are designed seem especially focused on curtailing expressions of abuse and depravity. Biblical descriptions of events in Eden, both before and after the first humans chose to experience immorality, starkly expose this purpose of the natural laws.

"Curses" on Humanity

The Garden of Eden was beautiful, bountiful, and comfortable. God optimally designed it to require relatively little maintenance. No thorns, thistles, or weeds grew there, and God designed natural sources to automatically water it. Moreover, all life in Eden— plants and animals—lived in harmony. Though Adam worked (see Gen. 2:15, 20) and likely experienced some sore muscles, his efforts and pain brought pleasure and satisfaction rather than agony and frustration.

Adam and Eve's choice to rebel against their Creator's authority and to experience evil firsthand dramatically altered the pleasures and fulfillment of Eden. From then on, God informed them, they would experience *more* pain and *more* work. To Adam God said:

> Cursed is the ground because of you;
>> through painful toil you will eat of it
>> all the days of your life.
> It will produce thorns and thistles for you,
>> and you will eat the plants of the field.
> By the sweat of your brow
>> you will eat your food
> until you return to the ground.
>
> Genesis 3:17–19

To Eve God pronounced:

> I will greatly increase your pains in childbearing;
>> with pain you will give birth to children.
> Your desire will be for your husband,
>> and he will rule over you.
>
> Genesis 3:16

God did not curse the world directly. There's no evidence to suggest alterations occurred in the physics of the universe or Earth. Few cosmic features could be more important for revealing their Maker than the constancy of the physical laws. If the force of gravity or the velocity of light changed occasionally, the result would be chaos and confusion (not to mention extermination). The universe would be indecipherable, at best, if each star and planet formed by different principles and processes.

The biblical prophet Jeremiah declared that the laws that govern the heavens and Earth are as "fixed," or secure, as God's promises to Israel (see Jer. 33:25–26). The apostle Paul said the entire universe (which would include all its space-time realm) is subject to the law of decay (see Rom. 8:18–23). Genesis stipulates that the sun and stars shone and creatures metabolized food both before and after Adam sinned (see Gen. 1:14–30; 2:8–17). Even the slightest change in the laws of physics would have drastically disrupted these (and other) vital processes.

Rather than the laws being changed, the ground became cursed as Adam and his descendants altered the manner of their work. Instead of wisely administering resources for the benefit of the plants, animals, and all life as God commanded (see Gen. 1:28–30), Adam and Eve and their descendants allowed greed, laziness, and selfishness to ruin their environment.

God's pronouncements on Adam and Eve and the ground were not only a judgment but also a warning. When humans practice evil, they experience additional pain and work. Extra work that serves no purpose but to partially reverse the effects of sin becomes "painful toil." This waste of valuable time and energy frustrates a person's ability to engage in more meaningful or pleasurable activities.

These verdicts apply to everyone. Male and female alike work harder and experience more pain, even in having children. The greatest torment is not in a baby's brief passage through the birth canal but rather in the emotional and spiritual anguish of a father and mother who anticipate and then watch their growing child making foolish choices and experiencing the painful consequences. Likewise, both husbands and wives struggle to sustain harmony with each other. The balance of authority and responsibility seems extremely difficult for any couple to maintain.

A Primary Purpose of the Physical Laws

No one enjoys seeing time wasted or being stuck with extra work or pain. The desire to avoid hardship is strong in every individual. This trait is so strong that parents, teachers, military officers, and governing authorities use extra work, pain, and wasted time as tools to correct unacceptable behavior.

Evidently, God designed the laws of physics so that the more depraved people become, the worse consequences they suffer. Such consequences impact not only the evildoer but also many others. Consider the damage done by an arsonist. Physics provides a powerful motivation (and leverage) for human authorities to limit expressions of evil. If the justice system fails to isolate and restrain the evildoer, many more individuals get stuck with extra work, wasted time, or devastating pain.

One critical difference between the discipline administered by physics and discipline delivered by human authorities is that human beings usually target the specific perpetrator of an evil deed. The most egregious crimes typically receive the greatest punishment, which can (or should) be carried out swiftly. However, human authorities do not successfully prosecute every crime. On the other hand, the laws of physics never fail to administer consequences for crimes committed. But the physical laws don't always target just the criminal and may not be swift in returning consequences.

As the Bible explains, it takes both natural consequences that arise from the physical laws and discipline from human authorities to adequately rein in humanity's impulse to commit evil. Further, as the Bible reveals and human observation verifies, unless human authorities are ever watchful, diligent, and just, and unless the physical laws consistently render consequences for wicked acts, evil will multiply. Physical laws help support the human system of justice. They also help explain why God may appear distant during natural disasters (see "Divine Rescue," p. 171).

Natural Consequences Curb Poor Choices

Physical laws not only discourage expression of harmful impulses but also encourage good behavior. Some personal examples illustrate how physics can assist human authorities to restrain evil and encourage individuals to do the right thing:

1. Rusty Tools

As the son of a machinist, early on I learned an appreciation for tools. Now my garage and kitchen are filled with them. My sons frequently borrow these tools to fix their gadgets. I have one request: return each tool immediately to its specific slot, hook, or drawer.

170

Divine Rescue

The Bible teaches that God is all-powerful, all-loving, and all-knowing. It also says that God is in complete control of everything that happens. Yet God often seems to be standing idly by while hundreds and even thousands of innocent people suffer or die from the ravages of a natural disaster. Why would a loving God who is also sovereign allow the forces of nature to shatter so many lives?

First, natural disasters really are, in one sense, "acts of God." In the context of the laws of physics and space-time dimensions, the forces behind such disasters are all designed to deliver significant benefit for humanity.

For example, God could easily eradicate hurricanes. Such elimination, however, would drastically reduce the input of sea-salt aerosols[1] and bacterial and viral particles[2] into the atmosphere. That reduction would lead to a decrease in rainfall. Hurricanes also regulate tropical ocean temperatures.[3] Given the laws of physics and space-time dimensions chosen for the universe, both the frequency and the average intensity of hurricanes are set to maximally benefit humanity and human civilization. Likewise, tornadoes, earthquakes, volcanoes, wildfires, ice ages, floods, droughts, and disease are all set at levels that deliver the maximum benefit and minimum damage to humans and their civilization.[4] But humans don't always make wise choices about where and how to build their dwellings.

Second, no human being can claim true innocence before God. All have sinned (see Rom. 3:9–12). All have defied God's authority in one way or another. All have fallen short of God's standard of moral perfection (see Rom. 3:10–20). So while people may be "innocent" of any specific offense related to the disaster they face, they are not innocent in any absolute sense that justifies accusing God of injustice.[5]

Third, God does not stand idly by. Often we're stunned at how many people survive nature's outbursts. We have no way to determine how catastrophic an event "might have been" apart from God's restraint. On some occasions it appears he miraculously intervenes to rescue people from disaster. However, if God intervened in natural calamities in an overriding way, he would abrogate their benefits, including the disciplinary benefits of physical laws and space-time dimensions.

What could explain God's "failure" to rescue all "innocent" people from criminal acts? If "good" people were never harmed by criminal acts or abusive treatment, human authorities might never take action to restrain evil or even to take evil seriously.

One day while pulling weeds in the backyard, I found three of my tools heavily encrusted with rust. A short time later, I enlightened my two sons as to how the laws of thermodynamics and chemistry operate: in less than a week, as they could plainly see, tools exposed to the elements, not to mention sprinklers, become so corroded that they no longer function efficiently. That loss translates into more pain, work, and time on the next occasion someone wants to use them.

My sons retorted that the pain and wasted time they might experience in the future would certainly be less than the pain and wasted time they experienced in listening to my lecture. I agreed as I handed them each a wad of steel wool.

2. Picking Cherries

The largest tree in the neighborhood where I grew up was a neighbor's cherry tree. It towered over the three-story homes and had a trunk four feet in diameter. Each summer it produced several hundred pounds of cherries.

One summer evening, just days before our neighbors intended to harvest the tree, they went out. After they left, about a dozen kids decided to steal all the cherries. Lacking proper ladders and cherry-picking equipment and not wanting to leave any cherries on the tree, they sawed off all the fruit-bearing limbs.

Those kids suffered some serious consequences for their misdeed. The first came quickly. They ate so many cherries in the process of committing their crime that most of them experienced severe pain in the gut.

Far worse, they and the whole neighborhood suffered long-term. The tree never recovered from the trauma, and the following winter it died. The entire group of neighbors, including the culprits who used to appreciate that tree, mourned the loss. No longer would it bless anyone with its beautiful blossoms, ample shade, and tasty fruit.

3. Clear-Cutting Mountain Forests

The home I grew up in had a wonderful view of several heavily forested mountains. One summer a logging company, eager for big returns on the sale of lumber, clear-cut the entire top portion of one of those mountains. That winter the suburbs at the mountain's base suffered their worst-ever floods and avalanches. The resulting soil loss stunted both the growth of the mountain's mid-altitude forests and the replacement forest on top.

4. Abusing Workers

One of my relatives worked as a broadcast and production engineer for a corporation headed by a compassionate leader. Employees and volunteers enthusiastically served the organization and often worked extra hours without being asked in order to assist the leader in fulfilling his vision.

When the kind leader died and his successor took over, everything changed. The new man insisted everyone, even volunteers, work long hours and often called them into work during off hours. His frequent midnight "brainstorms" meant his employees had to drop everything (or wake up) and join him at the studio. The employees' enthusiasm quickly evaporated.

Overall productivity and creativity plummeted. The abuse pushed employees and volunteers, subject as they were to the laws of physics, toward exhaustion and illness. Instead of getting more work out of his team, the new leader got less. Rather than looking for ways to further his cause, the employees and volunteers focused either on survival or on pursuit of employment elsewhere.

A Strong Deterrent

In all four examples, including the case of employee abuse, the laws of physics operated so that maltreatment resulted in more work, lost time, and added pain. For the offenders, the consequences provided powerful motivation to refrain from future wrongdoing. For those in authority over the wrongdoers, the consequences gave incentives to establish discipline and justice to curtail future misdeeds.

The optimization of the laws of physics to teach people how to make good choices is evident in the very high rate at which the law of decay propagates decay. Everyone has moments when they wish that law would generate less deterioration. However, for the laws of physics to effectively discourage poor choices and encourage right behaviors, the level of decay must be high enough to nudge us toward changed behavior. The rate at which the laws of physics generate degeneration appears just right: not so high as to discourage most humans from living productive lives but not so low as to offer little inducement to refrain from, and restrain, evil.

A Primary Purpose of Space and Time

The laws of physics are not the only feature of the universe optimally designed to restrain bad behavior. The space-time dimensions also are devised to keep the expression of evil in check.

Cosmic Time

Time limits wrongdoing because it is:

- unidimensional
- unstoppable
- irreversible

These characteristics of time mean no human can step outside of time, freeze time, or go back in time. They force humans into linear relationships. Choosing to spend intimate time with one person requires that others be left out. Cosmic time is designed in such a way that to build deep intimacy requires an exclusive level of focus. Marriage reflects that principle. So does friendship. Time limits people to just a few really close friendships.

While we might complain about how time prevents us from doing all we want, time does impose at least one beneficial constraint. Time limitations help restrict the amount of damage any one person can inflict on others—whether through gossip, lying, cheating, stealing, or something as extreme as assault or murder.

Less than a century ago, Adolf Hitler mandated the torture and execution of millions of Jews, but he planned even greater harm. Blaming the German people for the failure to fulfill his nightmarish dream, Hitler refused to surrender in the face of assured defeat.

Once he exhausted his pool of fighting-age men, he sent young boys and old men to certain death at the battlefront. He also refused to evacuate German civilians from cities and towns in harm's way. Hitler's time finally ran out, hastened by his own impatience and driven by an awareness of his impending death from Parkinson's disease (see "Optimal Life Spans"). As a result, millions of German and Jewish lives were spared.

Cosmic Space

The structure of cosmic space also helps keep wrongdoing in check. Three large, rapidly expanding space dimensions define humanity's current geography. This environment allows humans to be sufficiently close for relationships and yet sufficiently separated

Optimal Life Spans

The Bible's opening chapters (see Gen. 5:3–32, 11:10–32), as well as ancient Sumerian and Akkadian genealogies,[6] record early human life spans in the hundreds of years—as much as ten times beyond today's life expectancy.[7] In civilization's earliest days, long lives not only aided population growth but also facilitated the accumulation and transfer of knowledge. Unfortunately, the additional time also gave sin and evil increasing momentum to the point of threatening human extinction (see Gen. 6:5, 11–12).

Longer life spans prior to Noah's time as well as the localized concentration of human population (in the environs of Mesopotamia) allowed evil to spread like malignant cancer (see Gen. 11:1–9). With more time to inflict harm, the malevolent targeted and killed off the gentler, more virtuous souls. The end result: annihilation of *almost* all people who lived in reverence to God.

The Creator's drastic intervention, the Flood (see Genesis 6–9),[8] prevented humanity's total demise. God's coincident shortening of human life spans to a maximum of about 120 years (see Gen. 6:3) teaches an important lesson: longer life in a world where sin and evil abound does not serve humanity's best interest. The 120-year maximum life span is ideal. It's long enough for people to recognize their lack of goodness and turn to God, long enough for God-honoring people to establish a righteous heritage, and short enough to protect society from those who perpetually resist God and pursue evil.

for their protection. One reason Hitler and his henchmen couldn't carry out the slaughter of millions more people is that they could not *spatially* get to them.

In ordinary circumstances, if the object of a person's anger is not nearby, the anger often dissipates before its expression results in verbal or physical violence. Taking a clue from nature's laws and the cosmic space dimensions, human authorities—parents, teachers, and police, among others—use spatial separation (time-out or incarceration) as a tool to restrain destructive behavior.

Cosmic dimensions and physical laws also limit potential damage resulting from poor judgment, even amid attempts to do "good." When researchers began to understand that naturally occurring fires actually benefit forest ecosystems, national park fire management policies changed. Fires in the parks would now be allowed to burn. However, years of active fire suppression meant some areas had become dangerously overgrown.

In the summer of 1988, when lightning sparked fifty fires in Yellowstone National Park, authorities faced a policy dilemma. A year of severe drought meant they faced a horrific conflagration. So despite the new rule of nonsuppression, the nation's largest firefighting effort to date was launched. For three months firefighters fought valiantly as the flames wreaked havoc, devouring property and wildlife. Ultimately, it took weather, geography, and thermodynamics to help extinguish the inferno.[9]

Humanity's present space-time realm appears optimally designed to accomplish the Creator's multiple purposes. Its boundaries and limitations allow humans to relate to one another and to their Creator and at the same time serve to restrain disobedience of God's moral law and the expression of evil.

The End of Cosmic Physics, the End of Evil and Suffering

God created a confined cosmos within his unconfined realm to demonstrate the supremacy of his goodness and glory. Rather than scrapping this universe when Satan successfully tempted humanity to join his rebellion, God's plan was already in place.

Satan, to his own eternal outrage, still serves God's ultimate purpose.

Direct links between the laws of physics, including the cosmic space-time dimensions, and the conquest and permanent removal of evil are drawn in the pages of Scripture. These laws and dimensions are not evil. They have been in effect for 13.73 billion years but will not continue indefinitely. According to the Bible, a time comes when "creation itself will be liberated from its bondage to decay" (Rom. 8:21; see vv. 20–22).

That future moment arrives when the full number of God's children have received "redemption" (see Rom. 8:22–25). At that instant, the book of Revelation declares, Jesus Christ, the Creator and Redeemer, will intervene personally once again. An event referred to as the great white throne judgment will bring about the final and permanent end of evil (see Rev. 20:11–15).

With humanity's redemption and evil's end, this universe will have fulfilled all its purposes. No longer will there be any need for the restraints physical laws and cosmic space-time dimensions place on humanity. As God spoke the universe into existence (see Ps. 33:6, 9), he will speak it out (see Isa. 65:17; Rev. 20:11; 21:1–4).

Revelation describes the new creation that will one day replace the universe as a place without decay, death, or cause for grief or frustration (see Rev. 21:4). The descriptive details imply that neither gravity nor electromagnetism will exist there. As chapter 13 explains (pp. 194–203), the physics and dimensionality of the new creation will be radically different from the laws and dimensions governing the present universe. With evil forever gone, God will replace the universe with a realm that includes unlimited relationships, intimacy, love, pleasure, and fulfillment.

Ideal Stage for Redemption

The physics and dimensions of this universe simply help restrain evil. They do not conquer it or remove it. Likewise, humans can restrain evil, but they cannot eliminate it. As the Bible declares and every human conscience verifies, no one is perfectly good.

Every individual has gone astray in his or her own way (see Rom. 3:8–20). The more arduously a person attempts to live up to the moral standard dictated by conscience, the more frustrating the effort becomes and the greater that individual's awareness of his moral/spiritual shortcomings.[10]

Job, one of the most righteous men who ever lived, concluded that unless there were someone to intercede between God and himself, someone to make amends for his moral failings, he had no hope, no destiny (see Job 9:2, 14, 33; 10:14). And yet Job also concluded through his careful examination of the record of nature that the Creator is certainly powerful, wise, and loving enough to provide the means of redemption (see Job 9:4, 10; 10:12; 12:10). Thus Job trusted in the divine Redeemer to make amends for him and to conquer the evil that resided in his heart. He said, "Give me, O God, the pledge you demand. Who else will put up security for me?" (Job 17:3) and "My offenses will be sealed up in a bag; you will cover over my sin" (Job 14:17). Therefore, Job was able to declare with confidence: "I know that my Redeemer lives, and that in the end he will stand upon the earth. And after my skin has been destroyed, yet in my flesh I will see God; I myself will see him with my own eyes—I, and not another. How my heart yearns within me!" (Job 19:25–27).

Job put his trust in a future redemptive act by his Creator. Thanks to what the Bible and history record, people today can put their trust in the Creator's completed act of redemption. In studying the redemption story (see "God's Redemptive Act," p. 179), people also can discern how Earth, with its laws of physics and space-time dimensions, provides an ideal theater for the Creator to prove his moral perfection, model the humility and meekness required of us, pay the full penalty for our moral failure, and prove his power over evil, death, physics, and dimensions.

A Primary Purpose and Destiny for Humanity

According to the church's creeds[11] and Scripture's teaching, humanity's central purpose and destiny, both in the present and the new creations, is to "glorify" God (see Rom. 4:18–21; 15:17; 1 Cor. 10:31; Eph. 1:12–14; Col. 3:17; 1 Peter 4:11). That verb overflows

God's Redemptive Act

Through the early millennia of human history, God told of his promise and plan—available to everyone who places trust in him alone—to rescue humanity from an otherwise hopeless situation. He spoke through the voice of nature, through unmistakable interventions in nature (miracles), and through words he gave to human spokespersons (prophets). Then, at the moment of his choosing, he entered not just the confines of the cosmos but also the confines of a human body.

Fully human yet fully divine, Jesus of Nazareth accomplished what Adam and Eve (and we) could not. He resisted every enticement to act on his own, to depart from perfect obedience to the Father's will—even when suffering fatigue, hunger, ridicule, torture, rejection, and the horrible anticipation of carrying all humanity's sin into the moment of execution on the cross.

To assure us of his identity as Creator, Jesus demonstrated his power over nature's elements and laws—turning water to wine, walking on water, multiplying food, calming storms, restoring sight, curing disease, and even reversing decay and death. Jesus demonstrated his power over the supernatural as well, commanding demons (fallen angels) to do his bidding. He used Satan as a pawn, allowing him to incite religious leaders and corrupt politicians to carry out Christ's execution. In death Jesus fulfilled his ultimate purpose in coming—to suffer the full penalty for all humanity's sin, throughout all time and space, once and for all.

And the story doesn't end there. It continues because Jesus, God the Son, proved he is the door between the cosmos—with its space, time, matter, and energy—and a greater realm beyond. He passed through the grave clothes (cemented with at least 75 pounds of embalming spices; see John 19:38–40), through the sealed tomb (see Matt. 27:62–66), and into the Father's presence, not as an invisible spirit but in a tangible physical body. For seven weeks afterward, Jesus came and went from place to place among his friends and followers, sometimes hundreds at a time, physically real but unbound by space-time dimensions and the laws of physics (see Matt. 28:1–20; Luke 24:1–53; John 20:10–21:23; 1 Cor. 15:3–8).

Jesus could eat, but he didn't need to. He could walk, but he didn't need to. At his physical farewell, Jesus showed that gravity had no hold on him (see Acts 1:1–11). By his resurrection, Jesus triumphed over death and ascended into heaven to be with the Father. In that barely imaginable realm he prepares a place for us.

with meaning—exalt in praise, proclaim excellence, reflect splendor, express adoration. To give God glory is also to cooperate with him in the triumph of good over evil.

That God involves humanity in this ultimate purpose while clearly intending to rescue willing individuals from the cosmic limitations his purposes temporarily require establishes the high value he places on humanity and reveals the love he personifies. A combination of scientific evidences for humanity's hope and destiny (see chapter 7, pp. 108–17) and the theological perspective developed in this chapter help expose the fatal flaw in pessimistic conclusions concerning humanity's fate (see chapter 6, pp. 97–106).

Cosmologists' Oversight

Eddington, Jeans, Barrow, and Tipler in their anticipation of the universe's heat death (see pp. 96–97) and Krauss and Starkman in their depressing discussion of dark energy (see pp. 97–104) overlooked some significant data. These researchers concluded that humans and any other possible physical life in the universe must be without ultimate purpose or destiny. Yet from their own discipline of cosmology come discoveries that contradict the foundational assumptions on which their conclusions rest. Two of the more glaring faulty assumptions are that:

1. *"The cosmos is all that is or ever was or ever will be."*[12] The space-time theorems of general relativity, now established to an unprecedented degree of certainty, demonstrate the necessity of a causal Agent beyond space and time (see chapter 9, pp. 127–32). That means there must be another realm.

2. *Dark energy, which denies the possibility of hope within the universe, must not be real.* Recent observations (see chapter 2, pp. 36–40) from the Wilkinson Microwave Anisotropy Probe (WMAP) team, the Sloan Digital Sky Survey, and the Supernova Cosmology Project have confirmed the existence of dark energy beyond any reasonable doubt. These findings indicate that today dark energy is the universe's dominant component by far. Since it remains relatively constant throughout cosmic history and because dark energy dooms humanity's future within the cosmos, the source of our innate hope must reside in a realm beyond the cosmos.

Two Creations

Chapter 12 outlines one of the unique features of Christianity—the two-creation model of reality. While humanity's present home, the universe, was designed to facilitate a rapid and efficient conquest and removal of evil, the new creation will forever be free of evil and suffering.

A profound question, however, remains. Exactly how can the new creation be forever free of evil if it is filled with humans still in possession of free will? Chapter 12 explains how, in the context of two creations, this perfect realm can be possible without limiting humanity's free will or capacity to love.

12

Why Two Creations?

Like most teenage boys, my son Joel eagerly anticipated getting his driver's license. But his enthusiasm deflated when he learned the state of California forbids young drivers from transporting friends. His excitement took an even steeper nosedive when he discovered my buying him a new car was not part of the plan.

Joel's disappointment led him to consider alternate transportation modes, and the one that seemed most appealing was a motor scooter. Insurance was inexpensive, and at seventy miles per gallon he could go much farther on a dollar. During the two years Joel rode his metallic blue Yamaha Zuma, he learned a lot about the rules of the road and how to drive defensively. In many respects that scooter prepared him for the larger challenges of owning and operating a car.

In much the same way, this universe prepares humans for the new creation. The analogy breaks down, though, because the differences between the present creation and the new creation are vastly greater than those between a motor scooter and an automobile. And Christianity offers a radically different worldview—including its perspective on the world to come—compared to other religions.

An Unimaginable Realm

The creation myths of diverse cultures and ethnic groups bear remarkable similarities once they get to the part where humans enter the scene. Most tell of a human beginning in some kind of paradise. Then a conflict with gods or forces of nature breaks out and leads to the loss of that abode. From that time onward, humanity's quest is to regain the original splendor by appeasing the wrath of the gods/forces or by earning it through a system of good works or behavior management. The other alternative is to blot out all desire for what was lost.

In many creation passages, the Bible tells a different story (see appendix D, "Creation Accounts in the Bible," pp. 215–16). Rather than battling or appeasing God or gods to regain paradise lost (a realm resembling the conditions of the Garden of Eden), humans can anticipate a deliverance not just from the pains, evils, and sufferings of the present world but also from the limitations of the earthly paradise itself.

Christianity's new creation is a realm far beyond human ability to imagine. And in the current cosmos, God is *for* humans, not against them. He's provided for their pleasure and joy and promised to help them cope with life's challenges, including the effects of sin and evil. In the biblical view, trouble and trials prepare individuals to partake of a kingdom they wouldn't be equipped for otherwise. Those difficulties are not expressions of a deity's meanness, nor are they meaningless.

One problem humans face is that people can only visualize phenomena in the space-time dimensions they personally experience. For example, while mathematicians can prove that a basketball can be turned inside out in four independent space dimensions without making a cut or a hole in the basketball's surface, no mathematician or any other human can actually visualize the entire phenomenon. My professor showed us this possibility by presenting two dimensions of the four dimensions at a time.

This limited ability to visualize extra- or transdimensional phenomena can be a good thing. It provides a basis for testing the source of competing worldviews. Mere human inventions reflect this limitation. The paradise, or heaven, devised by a human mind will be humanly conceivable. However, a scenario (or model) inspired by a supernatural Source, such as the One who created space and time, would be expected to reveal a realm or realms beyond the capacity of any individual to visualize. Such a creation model would also reveal attributes of God beyond human capacity to imagine.

Distinct Differences

Christianity's two creations are radically different because they fulfill radically different purposes. The first is temporal, the second eternal. They do not overlap. No humans will inhabit the new creation until the present one is removed from existence (see Rom. 8:18–25; Rev. 20–22).

The first creation is "very good" (Gen. 1:31). It's the best possible realm to encourage as many people as possible to choose something far better: an eternal relationship with the Source of all goodness. This creation also equips and trains individuals to receive the roles, rewards, pleasures, and relational fulfillments of the new creation. It's the best possible place to bring about, part of that preparation, a rapid conquest of anything less than perfect goodness, and that of course includes evil.

The second creation is "perfect." Neither evil nor anything less than perfect goodness will ever exist there. Yet no limitation restricts anyone's free will. Consequently, love without limits can and will be expressed.

Sometimes skeptics challenge this two-creation model by asking, "Why didn't God just place Adam and Eve in the new creation to start with?" It appears that unless humanity is exposed to and tested by the greatest possible temptation, the most compelling attraction of evil, in the first creation—the rewards, pleasures, and relationships of the new creation cannot be made both perfect and permanent.

One Realm Makes Way for Another

A chronological outline reveals at least some of the connections between the Bible's two-creation doctrine and the enactment of God's triumph over evil:

1. God created the physical universe of matter, energy, space, and time. He also created angels.[1]
2. God "laid the foundations of the earth" (see Job 38:4, Ps. 102:25) and over several billion years miraculously shaped the planet and created hundreds of millions of different life-forms. He used all this life and a miraculous orchestration of its timing and features to prepare an optimally suitable place for humans, building up rich reservoirs of biodeposits for human civilization.[2]
3. The most powerful being God created, the archangel Lucifer (Satan), chose to rebel against God's authority and reject God's love. Satan enticed one-third of the angelic host to join his rebellion (see Rev. 12:1–9).
4. On Earth, God created Adam and then placed him in a beautiful, bountiful paradise, the Garden of Eden (see Gen. 2:7–8).
5. In Eden, God created Eve and brought her to Adam (see Gen. 2:21–22).
6. God allowed Satan to enter Eden in order to test Adam and Eve (see Gen. 3:1).
7. Satan tempted Eve first to distrust and then to defy her Creator (see Gen. 3:1–6). Eve, in turn, tempted Adam to distrust and defy God (Gen. 3:6, 12). In their act of defiance, Adam and Eve incurred "spiritual death" (see Gen. 3:7–8; Rom. 5:12–19). They attempted to hide from God and experienced the vastness of the gulf between his glory and their vainglory, a gap they could never cross on their own.
8. God took away the Tree of Life and ejected Adam and Eve from Eden. Having experienced spiritual death, they and their descendants would also suffer physical death (see Rom. 5:12–19). Their labor and relationships involved intensified pain, work, and wasted time (see Gen. 3:16–19).

9. God shortened the maximum potential life spans of humanity from 900-plus years to about 120 years (see Gen. 6:3).

10. God gave humanity a written moral code to complement the one already placed within the conscience of every person (see Rom. 2:14–15). These moral laws served to define goodness and expose the evil within every human heart, proving to all individuals their inadequacy to deal with and conquer their own propensity for wrongdoing.

11. At the precise moment of his choosing, the Creator of the universe confined himself to human flesh, allowed himself to be born of a woman, and grew up to manhood in a global crossroads, Israel. He lived there for a little more than thirty years. Jesus of Nazareth, fully God and fully human, served as a living, breathing example of moral perfection. He revealed his deity not only in words but also in expression of his power over all the forces of nature. Then, through his death on a cross, he made atonement for all of humanity's moral failures, all passive and active defiance of God. In rising bodily from the dead, he showed his sacrifice had been accepted and proved the tangible reality of a realm beyond the cosmos, even beyond physical death.

12. After Jesus's resurrection and ascension, God sent his Holy Spirit to personally indwell individuals who humbly receive Christ's payment and forgiveness in place of their own best efforts and worst deeds (past, present, and future), turning away from self-rule and submitting to God as the first and final authority in life (see John 16:5–15; 1 Peter 3:21; Eph. 1:13–14). With the consent of the surrendered individual, the Holy Spirit begins the process of transforming that person's mind, heart, and character to bring that person into a deepening and widening relationship with God (see Rom. 12:1–2).

13. The Creator prepares a new creation for all people who choose his offer of forgiveness and accept the terms of an eternal relationship with him, including consent to be transformed by his Holy Spirit (see John 14:2; Rev. 21–22).

14. Once the full number of individuals willing to receive God's offer of forgiveness and transformation has been reached,

God permanently removes them from this creation and removes anything less than perfect goodness (which of course includes all evil) from their presence (see Rom. 8:18–25; Rev. 20–22). Those people who receive God's gift enter his presence, an entirely different realm. Those who reject God's offer are forever sealed off, in an isolated and equally unimaginable place where, according to Revelation 20:12–13, expression of the evil in their hearts will be restrained, to whatever degree is necessary, by torment.

15. God brings all those who choose life into the new creation, the new habitat where they will dwell with God and one another for all eternity, free forever from sin and its consequences or even such a possibility (see John 14:1–4; Rev. 20–22).

This brief summary makes no mention of an era theologians refer to as "the millennium." Not all Christian scholars, pastors, or laypeople agree that Jesus Christ will reign on the present Earth for a thousand years in prelude to humanity's entrance into the new creation. Those who interpret Scripture this way describe the millennium as a period when God gathers in the last of those people who are willing to repent and receive Christ's offer of forgiveness and transformation. Conditions in this era, though presumably superior to humanity's current state, would fall short of what the new creation offers.

Eternal Freedom

Adam and Eve had a wonderfully intimate and loving relationship with God in Eden. At first there was no evil to mar that relationship, nor any wicked entity anywhere in the Garden, nor any collateral damage from evil.

Skeptics often ask, "Why didn't God keep it that way?" Or they may conclude the Christian God is too weak or uncaring to bother protecting his creation. According to the Bible, God certainly had the power to keep temptation away, but he was not content for humanity to experience an earthly paradise for the rest of eternity. He had better plans.

In Eden Adam and Eve lacked any assurance that their relationship with God, one another, and the rest of Eden's creatures would remain pure. God created the first man and woman as beings with free will. Human free will was crucial because without it, love is impossible. But to be truly free, a person's will must be tested by deliberate choices. So free will meant that at any time humans had the potential to go their own way, do their own thing, and worship something or someone less worthy.

For any individual to possess security in a relationship with their Creator, that relationship must be tested. The more arduous the testing, the greater the security. To ensure the possibility of eternally secure relationships, individuals endure the most difficult tests possible.

God left Eden's gate wide open on purpose. He made certain Satan and not some lesser demon approached Adam and Eve to tempt them. On purpose God permitted Satan to tempt Jesus of Nazareth as he was about to embark on his public ministry (see Matt. 4:1–11). God deliberately allows every human to be exposed to evil and its source in the spiritual realm. The apostle Paul explains: "Our struggle is not against flesh and blood, but against the rulers, against the authorities, against the powers of this dark world and against the spiritual forces of evil in the heavenly realms" (Eph. 6:12).

In God allowing Satan the opportunity to beguile humanity, God gave individuals the most difficult of all possible tests. No created being anywhere in God's creation is more powerful, appealing, or clever than Satan. If with God's help, an individual can overcome this great temptation, he or she can rest assured for all eternity that never again will there be a more difficult challenge than the one already overcome.

A Necessarily Arduous Process

A Ph.D. candidate's training provides a rough analogy. Candidates must first pass the most difficult courses in their discipline. Then they face the "comprehensives," which typically last all day.

Professors ply students with tough questions designed to test the depth of their knowledge and understanding. Once over this hurdle, candidates dive into research developing an original idea that significantly advances their chosen discipline.

Then candidates write a dissertation that exhaustively describes their findings. After review and appropriate revisions of that work, the students are ready to defend their work. A select group of professors pose challenging questions, usually for several hours. Candidates who provide satisfactory answers are awarded a Ph.D. degree.

Assuming the degree was earned honestly, it comes with two guarantees: the degree can't be taken away, and the recipient no longer needs to take courses or be tested to prove competency in their particular discipline. The basis for these guarantees is that those with a doctoral degree have already passed the most rigorous tests possible. Thus, they are granted a permanent seal of competency.

One other part of this analogy is relevant. In principle, the Ph.D. program is set at such a challenging level that even the most gifted and motivated of students cannot pass without expert assistance. Students who enter a Ph.D. program typically are excellent self-teachers. And yet some portion of the doctoral program is so difficult that they generally cannot master the course material and develop the appropriate research rigor and techniques without specific help from professors. Sadly, some students reject their professors' aid and consequently fail to reach their goal.

Life for every human is an arduous and enduring struggle against temptation. Unless a person accepts help from the all-compassionate Creator who is eager to help, that individual is doomed to fail. In passing life's most difficult test—choosing whom to trust and follow amid the most powerful distractions possible—an individual gains the assurance that never again will he face a test any more demanding. His choice is secure.

Transformed Will

The gradual transformation of desires and motivations that takes place when one bows to Christ as the master of life and invites the

Holy Spirit to metamorphose him into the image of Christ (Rom. 12:1–2, 1 Cor. 2:14–16, Col. 3:10) is another assurance of eternal security. There is no loss of free will in the process of giving one's life to Christ. The new believer continues to exercise free will in cooperating with, or resisting, the Holy Spirit in the transformation process.

The net effect of cooperation is the emergence of a pattern—increasing consistency in obedience to God, thus a growing reflection of godly character. The apostle Paul describes this effect as growing conformity to Christ's will (see also Rom. 7:15–8:17, 12:1–2; Eph. 1:11–14; Phil. 2:13; Col. 1:28–29).[3] By choice the captive makes such a practice of obedience that Christ's will in his or her life becomes strong enough to overcome the tug of personal autonomy with all its illusions.

The reverse is also true. One can become "captive to evil" by making a long-term and consistent pattern of rejecting God and his ways (see Rom. 7:15–25; 2 Tim. 2:22–26).[4]

A second reason that evil can never exist or be expressed in the new creation is that all new creation inhabitants will be captive to Christ's will. This does not mean, however, that those who enter the new creation have relinquished their freedom. Because of the manner in which God exposes humanity to evil and offers his assistance to overcome it in this creation, evil will no longer be possible in the new realm. God's plan is to use this universe to release those who choose life with him to a new level of free will and love far beyond anything ever experienced in earthly life. (Appendix E offers a brief clarification on how anyone can guarantee a place for himself in this perfect realm.) The apostle Peter wrote, "Praise be to the God and Father of our Lord Jesus Christ! In his great mercy he has given us new birth into a living hope through the resurrection of Jesus Christ from the dead, and into an inheritance that can never perish, spoil or fade" (1 Peter 1:3–4).

Chapter 13 reveals more about this glorious inheritance. It attempts to describe various features of the new creation as presented both explicitly and implicitly in Revelation—its geography, temporality, and physics in particular. The chapter leads to a portrayal of human life in the new creation and anticipates the role humans will fulfill there.

13

Why Is the New Creation Better?

A friend of mine once gave his mother a hammer designed for smashing her car's side window in case she ever crashed into a lake or river. With her "advancing" years, he wanted assurance she could get out of her car if it ever went under water. A month later, however, when riding with her, he couldn't see the hammer anywhere. When asked about it, she said, "Don't worry. It's in the trunk."

Unfortunately, a person can't get out of a car without opening a door or window. Nor can a basketball or an egg be turned inside out with its surface still intact—no holes, cuts, or cracks. These things may seem impossible, but as mentioned in chapter 12, a math professor once encouraged my class to watch a film demonstrating how one extra space dimension could permit such things to happen. The film illustrated this process by showing only two dimensions at a time, much like an architect displays a proposed house by drawing two-dimensional projections from various angular perspectives. Because humans are confined within four space-time dimensions, the human mind cannot form visual pictures of anything involving more dimensions or operating beyond our own.

That inability may explain why people struggle to envision the new creation—and themselves within it. God knows we need all the help we can get. So along with the gift of imagination, he made us insatiably curious. We are driven to explore, discover, and figure things out.

God also instilled in us a capacity to recognize and appreciate beauty and an intense desire to seek it out. Then he filled the universe with reflections of his majesty. As King Solomon said, "He has made everything beautiful in its time" (Eccles. 3:11).

Beyond Imagination

After his declaration about beauty, Solomon added, "He has also set eternity in the hearts of men; yet they cannot fathom what God has done from beginning to end" (Eccles. 3:11). If we humans—in spite of our education, wealth, and technology—cannot fathom the beauty and elegance in the creation surrounding us, how much more inconceivable is the splendor of the new creation!

In reference to our limited ability, the apostle Paul declared, "No eye has seen, no ear has heard, no mind has conceived what God has prepared for those who love him" (1 Cor. 2:9). Yet Paul exhorts us to do whatever we can to stretch our minds and strain our spiritual eyes toward that future so we can build a sustaining hope. He explains how this hope and confidence in our future life in the new creation is the best means to encourage one another and to motivate maturation and the development of godly character (see Phil. 3:7–4:1; 1 Thess. 4:18; 5:19–24; 1 Tim. 4:9–10; 6:11–16; Titus 2:11–14).

While no mind can fully conceive the magnificence of the new creation, God sprinkled glimpses of the life to come throughout the Old and New Testaments and planted exciting clues in nature's book as well. A quick review of these glimpses can increase our anticipation of the life to come.

Where "Up" and "Down" Are Located

Christian literature typically refers to heaven, or the new creation, as being "up" and hell as being "down." Given humanity's spatial context, some people conclude that hell must be down at

Earth's center or perhaps in space "below" Earth. Heaven is considered up and away in some distant part of the universe. Jesus's gravity-defying exit from his disciples' presence (see Mark 16:19; Luke 24:50–51; Acts 1:1–11) after his death and resurrection tends to reinforce this concept.

The Bible clarifies, however, that both heaven and hell continue after the moment God commands the cosmos to be "rolled up like a scroll" (Isa. 34:4), to "disappear with a roar" (2 Peter 3:10), and to "melt in the heat" (2 Peter 3:12). When the familiar space-time dimensions come to an end, "up" and "down" take on new meaning.

For now, the references to heaven as up and hell as down carry practical implications. Both realms exist in some spatial way and in some spatial relationship (or their equivalent) to one another in opposite directions, whether geographically, spiritually, or perhaps both. Picture two-dimensional creatures confined to a two-dimensional plane—stick figures on a piece of paper will do. Anything in the three-dimensional world would be "above" or "below" the stick-figure realm in dimensions they could not visualize.

A Matter of Time

Some Christian theologians refer to the new creation as a timeless eternity. In one sense they are right. Time as we know it will end when the universe ends because it is part of the created universe. However, the kind of phenomena and experiences time permits, such as cause-and-effect relationships, motion, emotion, and interpersonal interaction, do not end.

A "timeless eternity," devoid of anything remotely akin to cosmic time, would be static and eventless. But the Bible describes the new creation as alive with activity—events, travel, and meaningful relationships (see Rev. 21–22). Thus it seems more appropriate to describe the new creation as a time-*full* eternity. Some kind of "time," perhaps multiple time dimensions or super/supra temporal dimensionality (or the equivalent), must exist there. We can be certain that this new "time" will be different from and much less restrictive than cosmic time.

This fact brings great relief to people who grew up wondering and worrying about potential boredom in the new creation—one long day with singing and possibly playing the harp as the only activities. The Bible's detailed depictions of new creation physics dispel this misconception (see "Interpreting the Book of Revelation," below).

"Physical" Features and Laws

Revelation 21:4–5 says of the new creation, "The old order of things has passed away. . . . I am making everything new!" It appears order will continue because some type of orderliness, or consistency, flows from God's nature, but this feature will be expressed in entirely new ways. In particular, this new arrangement means "no more death or mourning or crying or pain" (Rev. 21:4).

The elimination of these experiences implies the law of decay (second law of thermodynamics) will no longer be in effect. Romans 8 echoes this change, saying, "the creation itself will be liberated from its bondage to decay" once the children of God have been "brought into the glorious freedom" (v. 21) of their "adoption" and "the redemption of [their] bodies" (v. 23).

One particular part of the new creation, the "New Jerusalem," is described in Revelation 21:10–27. These verses repeatedly contrast the Jerusalem and Zion located in Israel with the heavenly Jerusalem and heavenly Zion. Scripture frequently refers to the

Interpreting the Book of Revelation

Bible scholars agree that the book of Revelation includes symbols and symbolic language. They disagree, however, on the extent to which John uses symbols or analogies and on the interpretation of them.

My interpretive approach is to identify a passage in Revelation (or in any other biblical text) as symbolic only if its implied symbol is used and defined elsewhere in the Bible or if certain words within the context clearly indicate that the author intended something other than a literal meaning. It must be noted that "nonliteral" does not mean inaccurate or unreliable.

earthly Jerusalem as "the city of the living God" (Heb. 12:22)[1] and the mountain on which it resides, Mount Zion, as the place where God meets with man. They are places where God's people often fell prey to the evil influences around them. In the New Jerusalem and New Zion, everything is permanently and completely pure and righteous.

The apostle John's vision of the New Jerusalem includes measurements and dimensions. In Revelation 21 he observes an angel making length measurements using a rod and giving measurement results in cubits (see v. 17). A human cubit is 17.5 inches (44.5 centimeters) long.

The walls of the New Jerusalem are said to be 216 feet (66 meters) thick. The city's length, width, and height measure 1,380 miles (2,220 kilometers) each. The city has corners, implying that it is an enormous structure in the shape of a cube or perhaps a pyramid. Thus, some kind of spatial dimensionality (or its equivalent) must exist in the new creation. But gravity, mass, or both, at least as we know them, will not exist. (Gravity turns all massive bodies larger than about 300 miles or 500 kilometers in diameter into spherical shapes.) This detailed description implies that God crafts the New Jerusalem with precision and purpose.

John also describes being carried away in the spirit to an enormous mountain on the "new earth" where he witnessed the New Jerusalem descending out of the "new heavens" (see Rev. 21:1, 10). Given the New Jerusalem's dimensions, this "new earth" must be vastly larger than the present earth, with immensely larger geographical features.

In the new creation, structures can be built and inhabited without the limitations gravity and/or mass impose. Likewise, the size of inhabitable "planets" or geographical features seems unlimited.

The new creation will be bathed in light, but not electromagnetic light. No Sun, Moon, or stars will exist (see Isa. 34:4; Rev. 21:23; 22:5). There will be no need for lamps or any other familiar source of illumination (see Rev. 22:5). Nowhere within the new creation will there be any darkness, night, or shadows (see Rev. 21:23–22:5). Whereas darkness dominates the present creation, light will permeate the new. Whereas the majority of matter in the present creation absorbs and/or reflects light, everything in the new creation will radiate light.

In the present creation, all the physical laws are linked to thermodynamics, gravity, and electromagnetism. So the elimination of all three from the new creation implies the removal of *all* the physics that govern this universe. Totally new laws will take effect.

When God says, "I am making everything new," he apparently means all the physics and features of the new realm will be radically different from those we are familiar with. The end of sin and evil means physics will no longer need to set boundaries or to limit self-expression in work, creativity, play, and relationships.

Different Dimensions

New creation geography and measurements don't necessarily imply space dimensions. Superdimensions permitting spatial properties and much, much more may be the standard.

Spatiality in the new domain, whatever form it takes, certainly will provide more room for personal interaction than does the present creation. The physical laws and space dimensions of this universe restrict us to the surface. We live on the cosmic surface as well as on (or near) our planet's surface. Living much above or below Earth's surface results in serious health problems. In addition, economic limitations abound. For example, gravity makes the vertical movement of people, goods, and services in buildings higher than about 2,000 feet prohibitively inefficient and costly.

Such transport evidently is no problem in the new creation. A "mansion" with 750,000 "floors" (1,380 miles divided by 9.5 feet) would be neither impossible nor impractical. If those living in the New Jerusalem prefer ceiling heights adequate to accommodate Olympic downhill ski slopes, such features would easily fit—on each "floor."

Living space in the New Jerusalem will far outstrip anything imaginable on the present Earth (see John 14:2). Even with 40 billion residents, each person's "apartment" would be sufficient to accommodate a surfing beach, a mountain, a zoo, and a 36-hole golf course. In addition, people in the new creation will have access to a planet far larger than the present Earth, as well as to the "new heavens."

Most importantly, spatiality will no longer separate people. God promises a oneness with each other resembling his oneness as a triune God (see John 17:21).[2] This promise implies that humans will have all the room they could possibly imagine and yet never be so "far" from one another that they cannot have immediate and intimate contact with others at any "time."

Just as spatiality must be radically different, so too temporality must be radically different. For redeemed humans to be one—as the Father, Son, and Holy Spirit are—temporality must be multidimensional or the equivalent. When temporal experiences occur in the equivalent of two or more time dimensions (geometric instead of linear time), every human can have countless simultaneous interactions with others. No longer will anyone need to wait for an opening in anyone else's schedule. Each person in the new creation will be able to communicate with any other—relative, friend, Abraham, Moses, Mary, Martha, Lazarus, Paul, Peter, and best of all, God himself—without limitation.

Work

No activity will be wasted or meaningless in the new creation. Nor will anyone wonder about the purpose or significance of a particular task.

Paul writes to the Corinthians, "Do you not know that the saints will judge the world? . . . Do you not know that we will judge angels?" (1 Cor. 6:2–3). The Greek word *krinō*, for "judge," in this context means "to make determinations," "to resolve" in the sense that one sees a way through a complex challenge or problem, and "to rule, govern, and to preside over with the power of giving judicial decisions."[3] These definitions suggest that in some sense we will lead, instruct, and govern angels. Another Bible passage (Rev. 22:2) refers to "nations" in the new creation who are in need of healing. Thus, it is possible that redeemed humans will be ruling and instructing advanced creatures who are distinct from both humans and angels. The experience, education, and training we gain in this earthly life play a part, one way or another, in preparing us to fulfill and enjoy these different roles in the new creation.

The dawning of the new creation marks the unveiling of God's "eighth day" of creation.[4] His day of rest will have ended. God may have innumerable creation "weeks" mapped out for our future. If so, the "work" of redeemed humans could involve far more than anyone can now even begin to imagine. Such work can help us appreciate all the more our need for the training life here provides.

Prepared by Grace

Of all the experiences God gives redeemed humans to prepare them for the new creation, "grace" stands far above the rest. Grace refers to God's choice to treat us as if we deserve to be heirs of his goodness. In his mercy God refrains from giving us what our disobedient actions and evil inclinations warrant. He took that penalty himself as God the Son.

By grace God the Father allows those who abandon self-justification and embrace the full pardon he alone made possible to share fully in the inheritance of his "estate." All the inconceivably wonderful new creation rewards and pleasures are expressions of his grace. That inheritance includes work that is meaningful, gratifying, and enjoyable beyond what any earthly human can imagine.

Humans alone can experience God's grace. The angels only observe it. The Bible says the hosts of heaven intently observe us as they seek to comprehend the full impact of this grace (see 1 Cor. 4:9; 1 Peter 1:10–12). They watch us to grasp how "wide and long and high and deep is the love of Christ" (Eph. 3:18). As Paul explains, God's "intent was that now, through the church [redeemed humans], the manifold wisdom of God should be made known to the rulers and authorities in the heavenly realms" (Eph. 3:10).

Unlike the angels who joined Lucifer's rebellion, humans rebelled in a realm confined to four space-time dimensions and subject to the laws of physics. (Though not confined to our space dimensions, angels may be restricted to our time dimension.) Unlike the angels, humans are ruled over by a pervasive law of decay. When God ejected Adam and Eve from Eden and removed access to the Tree of Life, his grace already was unfolding. Physical death became a tool God could use for our ultimate benefit—a tool that did not exist for angels. Because of grace, redeemed humans will experience new creation rewards in a way angels cannot. Because of the ministry of God's grace, redeemed humans will gain occupations of the highest significance and delight.

Learning without Limits

Monkeys, apes, ravens, and jays express curiosity and learning capacity that is extraordinary among the world's creatures.[5] Yet their curiosity focuses on their immediate environment. It relates to their physical and social needs. Humans, on the other hand, wonder about everything: tangible and intangible, tiny and huge, near and far, the past and future as well as the present—the how and why of everything both in this universe and beyond. Human curiosity knows no boundaries, and many individuals will pay any price, even lose their own lives, to satisfy it.

One of life's great frustrations is the lack of time, resources, and technology—not to mention mental capacity—to research and comprehend all the things we hunger to know, not just about things but also about people. Whatever our interests, aptitudes, or resources, the universe's physics and dimensions place hard barriers on the quest to know and understand.

No more than we can fathom its beauty can we appreciate all God has done or will do in the realm to come. As King Solomon declared, "Despite all his efforts to search it out, man cannot discover its meaning. Even if a wise man claims he knows, he cannot really comprehend it" (Eccles. 8:17; see also Eccles. 3:11).

The present physical limits on our learning capacity will be lifted in the new creation. Furthermore, with total freedom from sin and decay, learning won't be a burden. It will bring joy. We will have continual access to the Master Teacher. Each of us will receive answers to the countless questions stored up during our earthly lives and the many millions more prompted by this new existence. We will enjoy intellectual, emotional, relational, and spiritual capabilities far beyond the apex of all we can ever experience on Earth.

Play and Rest

With current energy limits lifted, all our activities will be far more pleasurable than the most delightful recreations on Earth. What we now experience as "fun" will pale in comparison. We will never again encounter fatigue. Whereas here and now our anticipation of vacation may be dampened at least a little by various restrictions on recreation options—limits on time, finances, health, physical and mental endurance, and accessibility—the new creation will provide unlimited resources, time, and vitality. The fun will never end!

Relationship Pleasures

Much of the pleasure of working, learning, teaching, resting, and enjoying recreation involves the people with whom we do those things. However, it is also true that much of the pain and suffering we experience stem from some of those same relationships.

We have all met people, including Christians, who seem so different from us that we have no desire to be their intimate friends. All that will change in the new creation. The end of sin will be the end of pain and suffering in relationships. God will surround and fill every human with his presence and goodness.

Everyone will be taught by God (see John 6:45) and thus filled with knowledge and understanding. Each individual will be fascinating to communicate with, overflowing with kindness and compassion, and more attractive than we can describe or imagine. We will never encounter an obnoxious braggart, a dreadful bore, or a self-absorbed whiner. Each individual will radiate Christ's character.

Currently only a few people can share in the excitement of our favorite activities. Sometimes those with whom we would most love to share our joys are either too far away or too busy. But in the new creation all the time, space, matter, and energy restrictions will be gone. Never again will they keep any of us apart. Better yet, we won't need or want to be separated.

New creation physics will render marriage and family obsolete. God instituted these relationships to help us develop and experience maximum intimacy and nurture within the confines of cosmic physics and dimensions. These constraints mean that two people entering into marriage, as God designed it, focus a unique level of attention and energy on knowing and caring for the needs and interests of each other and share physical oneness with no one else. An intimate, growing bond between husband and wife provides the best possible environment for raising children. But, as in marriage, child-rearing success to a large degree depends on the parents' capacity to focus most of their care, nurture, and training on their own offspring.

In the new creation marriage and family take on an entirely new meaning. All of redeemed humanity will simultaneously experience closeness with God like that of a bride and groom. The Bible refers to our joyous meeting in the new creation as a marriage feast (see Rev. 19:7–9).

All of us will be family. Marriage and family relationships as we know them will be replaced by something so much more intimate, pure, and wonderful that we will never miss even the best of what we enjoy here, including sexual intimacy. Every human in the new creation will possess the capacity to maintain multiple simultaneous close relationships. Each of those countless simultaneous relationships will manifest a level of oneness that far exceeds the best, most intimate, most loving marriage that ever existed in the present creation, including Adam and Eve's union before they experienced shame. Never again will space, time, physics, or the effects of sin keep any of us apart.

Better Than . . .

No matter what new creation aspect we consider, every bit of it exceeds what any earthly eye has seen, ear has heard, or mind has conceived (see 1 Cor. 2:9). The biblical references to jewels, pearls, gold, and glowing light simply provide metaphors for something no earthly language can adequately express. Even those grossly inadequate metaphors, however, evoke a sense that the new creation's eternal rewards are so magnificent as to make our earthly troubles, as excruciating as they may sometimes be, seem trivial by comparison. The apostle Paul wrote in a letter to the Corinthians during an era of horrific persecution, "Our light and momentary troubles are achieving for us an eternal glory that far outweighs them all" (2 Cor. 4:17).

A vacation Kathy and I once took offers a miniscule glimpse of this concept. There were no roads into our destination—Mount Assiniboine Provincial Park in British Columbia. The closest we could get by car was nearly twenty miles away from the park. We planned to hike for two days to a campsite near the shore of Lake Magog, at the base of Mount Assiniboine. From there we would spend a few days exploring the park's peaks, glaciers, lakes, and meadows; then we would hike out.

With ten days' worth of food, our packs were heavy. Kathy labored under the weight of her load. Moreover, during the two-day trip, it never stopped raining. In most places the trail was several inches deep in mud. Copious quantities of horse manure mixed with the mud. But the worst misery of all, from Kathy's perspective, was the unrelenting onslaught of mosquitoes. Now, these weren't ordinary mosquitoes. Kathy claimed they were "the size of small birds."

It was uphill the whole way, and the last mile was especially steep. Kathy had managed to hold it together until that last steep mile up to the park boundary. All along the way we had seen some beautiful forests and meadows through the downpour, and that had helped. But that last mile was a killer—especially with mosquitoes now thicker than ever.

Only half a mile from the pass, Kathy announced that she had reached her limit. She could not take another step. We would have to turn back. She said she'd never felt more miserable in her entire life. Looking at her, I could see she meant it.

We had taken only a few steps back down the trail when Kathy said she needed to rest a minute, despite the bugs. After a few moments, she decided that because we were now so close, we should at least make it to the pass. It turned out I was wrong about the half mile. Actually, we were much closer.

Upon reaching the pass, we walked into sunshine. The mosquitoes, horse manure, mud, and bugs were replaced by a fresh breeze and firm path. Just thirty yards farther, we spotted a rock where we could sit with a view of the valley below and the peaks, lakes, meadows, and glaciers beyond. Kathy was stunned.

"I never imagined anything could be so beautiful! What are all those colors in the meadows?"

"Those are wildflowers and berries," I said. Then she noticed some dark brown forms moving about. "And those are elk," I explained.

"There's no way we're going back," she said, "at least not until our food runs out." Later Kathy told me that if she'd had a clue as to the wonders of Assiniboine, she would have complained a lot (or at least a little) less about the hardships of getting there.

That story shows only a microcosm of what we face in the new creation. God promises that *every* pain, grief, brutality, or indignity humans have ever endured in this realm will be more than compensated for by the magnificence, love, truth, life, significance, beauty, joy, and peace humans will enjoy in their new home. All the suffering and death the entire human race has endured, as great and horrible as it is, will seem "light and momentary" compared to the new creation's eternal rewards (2 Cor. 4:17).

All for Us

A few glimpses of the new creation rewards God will pour upon all humans who accept his redemption make all of his revealed purposes for this creation that much more understandable. How much the Creator has invested and will continue to invest for humanity's sake is astounding beyond all comprehension.

The Creator is also gentle and respectful. He will not force his gift on anyone who doesn't want it. Nevertheless, he challenges each individual to consider the magnitude of what he offers and what could be lost by refusing his generosity. As the author of Hebrews declares, "How shall we escape if we ignore such a great salvation?" (Heb. 2:3). (Appendix E, "Entrance to the New Creation," pp. 217–18 explains how to receive this wondrous gift.)

The Just-Right Vehicle

The universe was designed by God for his good purposes. It was not intended to last forever, and it is not meant to be our dream-mobile—but rather the perfect creation to carry us to our ultimate destination. Like eager children, we are inclined to ask again and again, "Are we there yet?" when most likely we still have a ways to go.

Occasionally we complain that someone else has a better view or that the seat belt is too tight. Then the driver reminds us to keep working on the puzzles he has given us. He knows that as we put the pieces together, we will continue to get a better understanding of his plans and discover more about the wonders of our destination. The trip is worth whatever time and effort it takes.

Biblical Basis for an Ancient Universe and Earth

Many scientists and others write off Christianity as a nonrational belief system because of the widely publicized notion that the Bible dates the origin of the universe and Earth at just thousands rather than billions of years ago. Purveyors of this notion vociferously defend it as *the* biblical teaching, and yet the majority of Christian scholars disagree. In fact, a literal and consistent reading of the Genesis 1 narrative alongside two dozen parallel or elaborative Bible passages (see appendix D) demands an ancient creation date, one that accords with the scientific data. The biblical case for an ancient creation appears in some detail in my book *A Matter of Days*. For a summary of that material, see the electronic compendium to this book at http://www.reasons.org/links/hugh/research-notes.

APPENDIX B

Where Is the Cosmic Density Fine-Tuning?

Jeff Zweerink and Hugh Ross

The "stuff" that makes up the universe must be fine-tuned in quantity and kind for the universe to manifest the expansion-rate history physical life requires. However, the fine-tuning source and fine-tuning degree depend on what kinds and quantities of stuff comprise the universe.

The dime illustration used on pages 35–36 is a word picture to demonstrate one part in 10^{60}. This number is used to quantify the fine-tuning of the cosmic mass density for life—assuming the universe contains only matter. If the density of matter is sufficiently large, gravity will eventually overcome the cosmic expansion and cause the universe to collapse on itself. If the density is sufficiently small, the cosmos will continue to expand forever with negligible slowing. At a specific density value in between, the universe will expand forever but at a continually slowing rate until the universe becomes static (at an infinite time in the future). In a universe that contains only matter, this particular density value corresponds to a "flat" geometry for the universe.

Life and flatness are related because only a geometrically flat universe meets two life-essential requirements. First, a flat universe survives long enough to form an adequate number of generations of stars to make the heavy elements and long-lived radiometric isotopes that are essential for advanced life (see chapter 3, pp. 43–55). Second, a flat universe expands slowly enough for the matter to clump together to form galaxies, stars, and planets but not so slowly as to form only black holes and neutron stars.

Until the mid-1990s, astrophysicists found it remarkable that the universe comes so close to having a flat geometry because such flatness tends to be unstable with respect to time. Back then they could only detect about 4 percent of the mass required to make the universe flat. Nevertheless, they were convinced that the early universe must have been *extremely* close to flat—to within one part in 10^{60}. This extraordinary fine-tuning holds true even given the uncertainties that existed twenty years ago (and still do to a lesser extent) in measurements of the cosmic mass density. Without such fine-tuning and without the existence of dark energy, the expansion rate would have changed so dramatically over time that the galaxies, stars, and planets necessary for physical life would never have formed.

Over the past fifteen years the picture has changed significantly. First, measurements of the radiation left over from the cosmic creation event, also known as the cosmic microwave background radiation (see chapter 3, pp. 53–56), confirmed that the universe is geometrically flat with an error bar (or measure of uncertainty) of about 2 percent.[1] Second, the concept of an extremely early epoch of cosmic inflation (a brief period of hyper-expansion of the universe when it was less than a quadrillionth of a quadrillionth of a second old) was developed into a scientifically testable hypothesis, which later measurements at least partially confirmed.[2] Third, astronomers discovered another density parameter for the universe, namely, space energy density or what is now known as dark energy.

For most astronomers and physicists, an early epoch of cosmic inflation solves the one part in 10^{60} fine-tuning "problem" because such inflation in the early universe drives the cosmos exquisitely close to a flat geometry regardless of its initial mass density. However, another fine-tuning problem remains.

The total cosmic mass density measured through several independent methods falls short by a little more than a factor of three from that required to make a flat-geometry universe. These measurements were established by the cosmic microwave background radiation (see table 2.1, "Inventory of All the Stuff That Makes Up the Universe," p. 37). Dark energy (the space energy density) makes up the deficit, but not without a price.

By any accounting, the source or sources of dark energy are at least 120 orders of magnitude larger than the amount detected. This difference implies that somehow the source(s) must cancel so as to leave only one part in 10^{120} in order to match the small amount of dark energy detected by astronomers. Therefore, while inflation and dark energy can dramatically reduce the one part in 10^{60} fine-tuning in the mass density of the universe, they can do so only by introducing the far more exquisite one part in 10^{120} fine-tuning in the dark energy density.

In other words, the exquisite fine-tuning remains inescapable.

APPENDIX C

Designed for Life

A catalog of characteristics of the universe and Earth that require fine-tuning for life's existence, including relevant citations to the scientific literature, is available as an electronic compendium to this book and may be accessed at http://www.reasons.org/links/ hugh/research-notes. This catalog includes four parts:

Part 1: Fine-Tuning for Life in the Universe—lists 140 features of the cosmos as a whole (including the laws of physics) that must fall within certain narrow ranges to make physical life possible.

Part 2: Fine-Tuning for Intelligent Physical Life—describes 402 quantifiable characteristics of a planetary system and its galaxy that must fall within narrow ranges to make advanced life possible. This list also explains in each case how the slight increase or decrease in the value of the characteristic would destroy the possibility for advanced life's existence.

Part 3: Probability Estimates for the Features Required by Various Life-Forms—identifies 824 characteristics of a galaxy and of a planetary system that make physical life possible and gives estimates of the probability that a galaxy and planetary system would manifest such characteristics. This list is broken down into the fine-tuning requirements for various kinds of life.

Part 4: Probability Estimates on Different Size Scales for the Features Required by Advanced Life—presents a breakdown of the 824 characteristics as they arise, separately, from the galaxy cluster, galaxy, planetary system, planet, planet's surface, and planet's other life.

APPENDIX D

Creation Accounts in the Bible

Among all books deemed "holy," the Bible speaks by far the most extensively about the natural world, how it works, and how (as well as why) it came to be. Thousands of biblical verses and passages make reference to scientifically testable concepts. In addition to these brief references, the Bible contains multiple chapter-length or longer treatments of topics relevant to creation and science. Those texts and the themes addressed include:

Text	Theme
Genesis 1	Creation chronology: a physical perspective
Genesis 2	Creation account: a spiritual perspective
Genesis 3–5	Human sin and its damage
Genesis 6–9	God's damage-control response to sin
Genesis 10–11	Global dispersion of humanity
Job 9	Creator's transcendent power
Job 34–41	Creation's intricacy and complexity
Psalm 8	Creation's reminder of our humility

Text	Theme
Psalm 19	Creation's ubiquitous "speech"
Psalm 33	God's love as revealed in creation
Psalm 65	Creator's authority and optimal provision
Psalm 104	Elaboration of physical creation events
Psalm 139	Creation of individual humans
Psalms 147–48	Nature's testimony to the Creator's power, wisdom, and care
Proverbs 8	Creator's existence before creation
Ecclesiastes 1–2	Constancy of the physical laws
Ecclesiastes 3	Chronology in creation
Ecclesiastes 8–12	God's purpose and humanity's destiny
Isaiah 40–51	Origin and development of the universe
Romans 1–8	God's purposes in creating
1 Corinthians 15	Life after life
2 Corinthians 4	Creator's glory in and beyond creation
Hebrews 1	Cosmic creation's temporality; role of angels in creation
Hebrews 4	God's rest and work
2 Peter 3	Present creation's end
Revelation 19–20	End of evil, decay, and death; end of the present creation
Revelation 21–22	The new creation's wonders

APPENDIX E

Entrance to the New Creation

The "good news" of the books referred to as the Gospels (Matthew, Mark, Luke, and John) is that Jesus of Nazareth, the Creator of the universe, came in person to lead people into the new creation. Whoever answers the call to follow him can enter the transcendent realm for which he destined us. When Christ's earthly friends asked for clear directions to get there, he replied unambiguously, "I am the way and the truth and the life. No one comes to the Father except through me" (John 14:6).

No alternate routes, no shortcuts, and no ways around him exist.

What exactly does it mean to follow Jesus, to come "through" him? It means to exercise the desire and power he alone can provide to:

Repent	of your sin, specifically of going your own way through life as if you're in charge, as if you're the judge of right and wrong and can determine what's good enough to please God. In other words, you must admit to God that he alone holds authority over your life and then relinquish judgment to him.

Believe through study and testing that Jesus of Nazareth is exactly the person he claimed to be—fully God and fully human—the only being who could actually *be* good in actions, words, and thoughts. Believe that because he did nothing to deserve death, his execution covered the penalty for all your sin, your lack of perfect goodness in actions, words, and thoughts. And believe that God accepted his sacrifice in your place, raising him bodily from the grave.

Commit your life to learning day by day what it means to follow him; to love him with all your heart, soul, mind, and strength; and to love others as yourself. Acknowledge the gift of his Holy Spirit within you, and trust him to nurture your growth as you live in the community of other Christ followers. Trust him to help you release anything, such as bitterness or unforgiveness, that hinders your growth.

Speak Up in words and actions to let others know you are a follower of Jesus—and why. Invite them to come along with you in a lifelong journey. It will be full of challenges. You will encounter great joys and sorrows, delights and sufferings, but never without God's comfort and care. And when you enter the new creation, everything will make sense. It will all be worthwhile.

Notes

Introduction: Let's Play "I Spy"

1. Stephen W. Hawking, *A Brief History of Time: From the Big Bang to Black Holes* (New York: Bantam, 1988), 127.

2. Freeman J. Dyson, *Disturbing the Universe* (New York: Basic, 1979), 250.

3. For the original quote, see Albert Einstein, "Physics and Reality" (1936), in *Ideas and Opinions*, trans. Sonja Bargmann (New York: Bonanza, 1954), 292.

Chapter 1: Why Ask *Why* Questions?

1. Hawking, *A Brief History of Time*, 171.

2. See, for example, Immanuel Kant, "Universal Natural History and Theory of the Heavens," trans. W. Hastie, in *Theories of the Universe: From Babylonian Myth to Modern Science*, ed. Milton K. Munitz (New York: Free Press, 1957), 240; Giordano Bruno, "On the Infinite Universe and Worlds," in *Theories of the Universe*, 174–83; John North, *The Norton History of Astronomy and Cosmology* (New York: Norton, 1995), 374–79.

3. See Hugh Ross, *The Creator and the Cosmos: How the Greatest Scientific Discoveries of the Century Reveal God*, 3rd ed. (Colorado Springs: NavPress, 2001); Hugh Ross, *Beyond the Cosmos: The Extra-Dimensionality of God; What Recent Discoveries in Astrophysics Reveal about the Glory and Love of God*, 2nd ed. (Colorado Springs: NavPress, 1999); Hugh Ross, *Creation as Science: A Testable Model Approach to End the Creation/Evolution Wars* (Colorado Springs: NavPress, 2006), 66–83, 85–117.

4. For an explanation as to why interstellar space travel by physical intelligent beings defies the laws of physics, see Hugh Ross, Kenneth Samples, and Mark

Clark, *Lights in the Sky and Little Green Men: A Rational Christian Look at UFOs and Extraterrestrials* (Colorado Springs: NavPress, 2002), 55–64.

5. For a well-known early example, see Augustine, *The Literal Meaning of Genesis*, trans. and annotated by John Hammond Taylor, bk. 4, chap. 33–34, and bk. 5, chap. 3, in vol. 41 of *Ancient Christian Writers: The Works of the Fathers in Translation*, ed. Johannes Quasten, Walter J. Burghardt, and Thomas C. Lawler (New York: Newman, 1982), 141–45, 149–50.

6. Fang Li Zhi and Li Shu Xian, *Creation of the Universe*, trans. T. Kiang (Singapore: World Scientific, 1989), 173.

7. Hawking, *Brief History of Time*, 13.

8. Ibid., 169.

9. Ibid., 175.

Chapter 2: Why Such a Vast Universe?

1. Victor J. Stenger, *God: The Failed Hypothesis: How Science Shows That God Does Not Exist* (Amherst, NY: Prometheus, 2007), 156.

2. Stephen W. Hawking, *A Brief History of Time*, 126.

3. Stenger, *God*, 157.

4. Ibid.

5. Steven V. W. Beckwith et al., "The Hubble Ultra Deep Field," *Astronomical Journal* 132 (November 2006): 1729–55.

6. See Hugh Ross, *The Creator and the Cosmos*, 124.

7. See Masataka Fukugita and P. J. E. Peebles, "The Cosmic Energy Inventory," *Astrophysical Journal* 616 (December 2004): 643–68; D. N. Spergel et al., "Three-Year *Wilkinson Microwave Anisotropy Probe (WMAP)* Observations: Implications for Cosmology," *Astrophysical Journal Supplement Series* 170 (June 2007): 377–408.

8. See Peter Coles and George F. R. Ellis, *Is the Universe Open or Closed? The Density of Matter in the Universe* (Cambridge: Cambridge University Press, 1997); Peter Coles, ed., *The Routledge Critical Dictionary of the New Cosmology* (New York: Routledge, 1998), 180–83; Lawrence M. Krauss, "The End of the Age Problem and the Case for a Cosmological Constant Revisited," *Astrophysical Journal* 501 (July 10, 1998): 461, 465.

9. Fukugita and Peebles, "Cosmic Energy Inventory," 643–68.

10. Spergel et al., "Three-Year *Wilkinson Microwave Anisotropy Probe (WMAP)* Observations," 377–408. E. Komatsu et al., "Five-Year Wilkinson Microwave Anisotropy Probe (WMAP) Observations: Cosmological Interpretation" (preprint, National Aeronautics and Space Administration, 2008): http://lambda.gsfc.nasa .gov/product/map/dr3/pub_papers/fiveyear/cosmology/wmap_5yr_cosmo.pdf.

11. North, *Norton History of Astronomy and Cosmology*, 502–7; P. J. E. Peebles, *Principles of Physical Cosmology* (Princeton, NJ: Princeton University Press, 1993), 417.

12. Morton S. Roberts, "The Content of Galaxies: Stars and Gas," in *Annual Review of Astronomy and Astrophysics*, ed. Leo Goldberg, Armin J. Deutsch, and David Layzer (Palo Alto, CA: Annual Reviews, 1963), 160–63; J. H. Oort, "Stellar Dynamics," in *Galactic Structure*, ed. Adriaan Blaauw and Maarten Schmidt

(Chicago: University of Chicago Press, 1965), 469–73; Rudolf Kippenhahn and Alfred Weigert, *Stellar Structure and Evolution*, corrected printing (New York: Springer-Verlag, 1994), 268.

13. Kippenhahn and Weigert, *Stellar Structure and Evolution*, 215, 266–69.

14. Ruth A. Daly and S. G. Djorgovski, "Direct Determination of the Kinematics of the Universe and Properties of the Dark Energy as Functions of Redshift," *Astrophysical Journal* 612 (September 10, 2004): 652–59; Ruth A. Daly et al., "Improved Constraints on the Acceleration History of the Universe and the Properties of the Dark Energy," *Astrophysical Journal* 677 (April 10, 2008): 1–11.

15. For a more thorough analysis of the demise of the oscillating universe model and of the Hindu/Buddhist/new age concept of a reincarnating universe, see Ross, *Creator and the Cosmos*, 48–67, 87–98, 169–74.

16. Bradley E. Schaefer, "The Hubble Diagram to Redshift >6 from 69 Gamma-Ray Bursts," *Astrophysical Journal* 660 (May 2007): 16–46; Uros Seljak, Anze Slosar, and Patrick McDonald, "Cosmological Parameters from Combining the Lyman-α Forest with CMB, Galaxy Clustering and SN Constraints," *Journal of Cosmology and Astroparticle Physics* 10 (October 19, 2006): 014.

17. Lawrence M. Krauss, *Quintessence: The Mystery of the Missing Mass* (New York: Basic, 2000), 103–5; Krauss, "End of the Age Problem," 461, 465.

Chapter 3: Why Such an Old Universe?

1. E. Komatsu et al., "Five-Year Wilkinson Anisotropy Probe (WMAP) Observations: Cosmological Interpretation," *Astrophysical Journal Supplement Series* (2008): in press.

2. Peter D. Ward and Donald Brownlee, *Rare Earth: Why Complex Life Is Uncommon in the Universe* (New York: Copernicus/Springer-Verlag, 2000), 191–220; Hugh Ross, *Creation as Science: A Testable Model Approach to End the Creation/Evolution Wars* (Colorado Springs: NavPress, 2006), 104.

3. Ward and Brownlee, *Rare Earth*, 29, 194, 212–13.

4. I explain this compensation in *Creation as Science*, 129–38.

5. Joel Baker et al., "Early Planetesimal Melting from an Age of 4.5662 Gyr for Differentiated Meteorites," *Nature* 436 (August 25, 2005): 1127–31; C. J. Allègre, G. Manhès, and C. Göpel, "The Age of the Earth," *Geochimica et Cosmochimica Acta* 59 (April 1995): 1445–56.

6. Two modern-day examples of highly radiation-resistant bacterial species are *Bacillus subtilis* and *Deinococcus radiodurans*. The latter bacterium can survive 500 times more radiation than a human can.

7. M. W. Caffee et al., "Evidence in Meteorites for an Active Early Sun," *Astrophysical Journal Letters* 313 (February 1, 1987): L31–L35; M. W. Caffee et al., "Irradiation Records in Meteorites," in *Meteorites and the Early Solar System*, ed. J. F. Kerridge and M. S. Matthews (Tucson: University of Arizona Press, 1988), 205–45; Daniel P. Whitmire et al., "A Slightly More Massive Young Sun as an Explanation for Warm Temperatures on Early Mars," *Journal of Geophysical Research* 100 (March 1995): 5457–64; J. Geiss, "Solar Wind Composition and Implications about the History of the Solar System," in *Proceedings of the 13th International Cosmic Ray Conference*, vol. 5, ed. R. L. Chasson (Denver: University of Denver

Press, 1973), 3375–98; J. Geiss and P. Bochsler, "Long Time Variations in Solar Wind Properties: Possible Causes Versus Observations," in *The Sun in Time*, ed. C. P. Sonett, M. S. Giampapa, and M. S. Matthews (Tucson: University of Arizona Press, 1991), 98–117; J. F. Kerridge et al., "Long-Term Changes in Composition of Solar Particles Implanted in Extraterrestrial Materials," in *The Sun in Time*, 389–412; Brian E. Wood et al., "Observational Estimates for the Mass-Loss Rates of α Centauri and Proxima Centauri Using *Hubble Space Telescope* Lyα Spectra," *Astrophysical Journal Letters* 547 (January 20, 2001): L49–L52.

8. I. Juliana Sackmann and Arnold I. Boothroyd, "Our Sun. V. A Bright Young Sun Consistent with Helioseismology and Warm Temperatures on Ancient Earth and Mars," *Astrophysical Journal* 583 (February 1, 2003): 1024–39.

9. Kippenhahn and Alfred Weigert, *Stellar Structure and Evolution*, 277–80.

10. Ross, *Creation as Science*, 125–47.

11. Donald E. Canfield and Andreas Teske, "Late Proterozoic Rise in Atmospheric Oxygen Concentration Inferred from Phylogenetic and Sulfur-Isotope Studies," *Nature* 382 (July 11, 1996): 127–32; Donald E. Canfield, "A New Model for Proterozoic Ocean Chemistry," *Nature* 396 (December 3, 1998): 450–53; John M. Hayes, "A Lowdown on Oxygen," *Nature* 417 (May 9, 2002): 127; Paul G. Falkowski et al., "The Rise of Oxygen over the Past 205 Million Years and the Evolution of Large Placental Mammals," *Science* 309 (September 30, 2005): 2202–4.

12. The Bible accurately predicted the features shown in figure 3.5 thousands of years before scientists discovered them. Genesis 1:2 says water covered the entire surface of early Earth, apparently before the origin of Earth's first life. Genesis 1:9–10 seems to place the most dramatic buildup of continental landmasses when Earth reached about half its present age, most likely at the beginning of creation day three.

13. E. Komatsu et al., "Five-Year Wilkinson Microwave Anisotropy Probe (WMAP) Observations: Cosmological Interpretation," (preprint, National Aeronautics and Space Administration, 2008): http://lambda.gsfc.nasa.gov/product/map.dr3/pub_papers/fiveyear/cosmology/wmap_5yr_cosmo.pdf; L. Page et al., "Three-Year *Wilkinson Microwave Anisotropy Probe (WMAP)* Observations: Polarization Analysis," *Astrophysical Journal Supplement Series* 170 (June 2007): 335–76; D. N. Spergel et al., "Three-Year *Wilkinson Microwave Anisotropy Probe (WMAP)* Observations: Implications for Cosmology," *Astrophysical Journal Supplement Series* 170 (June 2007): 377–408.

14. For how the big bang fused nearly 25 percent of the universe's hydrogen into helium during the first four minutes of cosmic existence, see my article "Primordial Helium Abundance Test of Big Bang Cosmology," Reasons To Believe, November 26, 2007, http://www.reasons.org/tnrtb/2007/11/page/2/.

15. Lawrence M. Krauss and Robert J. Scherrer, "The Return of a Static Universe and the End of Cosmology," *General Relativity and Gravitation* 39 (October 2007): 1545–50.

Chapter 4: Why Such a Lonely Universe?

1. This statement was reconstructed from Los Alamos National Laboratory physicist Eric M. Jones's personal interviews of Teller, Konopinski, and York

concerning their recollection of the luncheon conversation with Fermi. Eric M. Jones, "Where Is Everybody? An Account of Fermi's Question," *UFO Evidence*, http://www.ufoevidence.org/documents/doc1057.htm (accessed September 19, 2007). Additional articles concerning Fermi's paradox can be found at *UFO Evidence*, http://www.ufoevidence.org/topics/fermi.htm (accessed September 19, 2007).

2. Ross, Samples, and Clark, *Lights in the Sky*, 33–71, 99–192.

3. The 250-light-year minimum trip assumes that an intelligent species capable of interstellar space travel exists just beyond the 200 light-year distant region from Earth that Project Phoenix has ascertained is devoid of any species as technologically advanced as humans on Earth today. However, navigating a spaceship through the benign regions of interstellar space, that is, avoiding major interstellar hazards, will add at least another 50 light-years to the trip.

4. Ross, Samples, and Clark, *Lights in the Sky*, 61–63.

5. The same thing could be said about the Mars Mission Simulation conducted during the summer of 2007 in the Canadian arctic. The seven scientists in the Flashline Mars Arctic Research Station lived in a small two-story capsule for one hundred days. However, they were not confined to the capsule. They conducted regular snowmobile trips to nearby lakes and rock outcroppings and received supplies on a regular basis from the outside. For details see The Mars Society, http://www.fmars2007.org (accessed December 4, 2007).

6. William Speed Weed, "Can We Go to Mars without Going Crazy?" *Discover*, May 2001, 38.

7. P. R. Backus and Project Phoenix Team, "Project Phoenix: A Summary of SETI Observations and Results, 1995–2004," American Astronomical Society Meeting 204, #75.04, *Bulletin of the American Astronomical Society* 36 (May 2004): 805; Ian Morison, "SETI in the New Millennium," *Astronomy & Geophysics* 47 (August 2006): 4.12–4.16; Wikipedia contributors, "SETI," *Wikipedia: The Free Encyclopedia*, http://en.wikipedia.org/wiki/SETI (accessed September 19, 2007).

8. For descriptions of how the solar system's gas giant planets protect Earth from receiving too many comet and asteroid collisions, see Jeff Zweerink, "Jupiter, Friend or Foe?" Reasons To Believe, November 7, 2007, http://www.reasons.org/tnrtb/2007/11/page/6/; and Dave Rogstad, "Two Steps Forward, One Step Back," Reasons To Believe, September 28, 2007, http://www.reasons.org/tnrtb/2007/09/.

9. *The Extrasolar Planets Encyclopaedia*, s.v. "Interactive Extra-Solar Planets Catalog," http://vo.obspm.fr/exoplanetes/encyclo/catalog-RV.php (accessed September 25, 2007).

10. Jorge Meléndez, Katie Dodds-Eden, and José A. Robles, "HD 98618: A Star Closely Resembling Our Sun," *Astrophysical Journal Letters* 641 (April 20, 2006): L133; http://www.reasons.org/tnrtb/2008/03/17/.

11. Interested readers will find a description and explanation of these early Greek proofs in Hugh Ross, *The Fingerprint of God: Recent Scientific Discoveries Reveal the Unmistakable Identity of the Creator*, 2nd ed. (Orange, CA: Promise, 1991), 12–15.

12. Fukugita and Peebles, "The Cosmic Energy Inventory," 643–68.

13. B. Evardsson et al., "The Chemical Evolution of the Galactic Disk. I. Analysis and Results," *Astronomy and Astrophysics* 275 (August 1993): 101–52;

Guillermo Gonzalez, "Solar System Bounces in the Right Range for Life," *Facts & Faith*, first quarter 1997, 4.

14. Guillermo Gonzalez, Donald Brownlee, and Peter Ward, "The Galactic Habitable Zone: Galactic Chemical Evolution," *Icarus* 152 (July 2001): 185–200; M. Sundin, "The Galactic Habitable Zone in Barred Galaxies," *International Journal of Astrobiology* 5 (September 2006): 325–26; Guillermo Gonzales, "The Galactic Habitable Zone," in *Astrophysics of Life*, ed. Mario Livio, I. Neill Reid, and William B. Sparks (Cambridge: Cambridge University Press, 2005), 89–97; Charles H. Lineweaver, Yeshe Fenner, and Brad K. Gibson, "The Galactic Habitable Zone and the Age Distribution of Complex Life in the Milky Way," *Science* 303 (January 2, 2004): 59–62; Guillermo Gonzalez and Jay Richards, *Privileged Planet: How Our Place in the Cosmos Is Designed for Discovery* (Washington, DC: Regnery, 2004), 143–68.

15. D. L. Block et al., "An Almost Head-On Collision as the Origin of Two Off-Centre Rings in the Andromeda Galaxy," *Nature* 443 (October 19, 2006): 832–34.

16. F. Hammer et al., "The Milky Way, An Exceptionally Quiet Galaxy: Implications for the Formation of Spiral Galaxies," *Astrophysical Journal* 682 (June 10, 2007): 322–34.

17. The earliest one of those books was one Sagan coauthored with the Russian astrophysicist I. S. Shklovskii, *Intelligent Life in the Universe* (San Francisco: Holden-Day, 1966). The discussion about life's origin is on page 237.

18. About 3.85 billion years ago, a very heavy bombardment of asteroids and comets turned the entire surface of Earth into a molten lava state at 3,000 degrees centigrade and at least 200 kilometers deep. Not until about 3.80 billion years ago did Earth cool enough for rocks and liquid water to form. However, carbon isotope analysis confirms that life was abundant on Earth as far back as about 3.80 billion years ago. Therefore, life must have arisen on Earth within a few million years or less. For details and citations to the original research findings see Fazale Rana and Hugh Ross, *Origins of Life: Biblical and Evolutionary Models Face Off* (Colorado Springs: NavPress, 2004), 81–105.

19. Minik T. Rosing, "^{13}C-Depleted Carbon Microparticles in >3700–Ma Sea-Floor Sedimentary Rocks from West Greenland," *Science* 283 (January 29, 1999): 674–76; S. J. Mojzsis et al., "Evidence for Life on Earth before 3,800 Million Years Ago," *Nature* 384 (November 7, 1996): 55–59; John M. Hayes, "The Earliest Memories of Life on Earth," *Nature* 384 (November 7, 1996): 21–22; Manfred Schidlowski, "A 3,800-Million-Year Isotopic Record of Life from Carbon in Sedimentary Rocks," *Nature* 333 (May 26, 1988): 313–18; Daniele L. Pinti, Ko Hashizume, and Jun-ichi Matsuda, "Nitrogen and Argon Signatures in 3.8 to 2.8 Ga Metasediments: Clues on the Chemical State of the Archean Ocean and the Deep Biosphere," *Geochimica et Cosmochimica Acta* 65 (July 1, 2001): 2309; V. Beaumont and F. Robert, "Nitrogen Isotope Ratios of Kerogens in Precambrian Cherts: A Record of the Evolution of Atmosphere Chemistry?" *Precambrian Research* 96 (June 15, 1999): 63–82; Jay A. Brandes et al., "Abiotic Nitrogen Reduction on the Early Earth," *Nature* 395 (September 24, 1998): 365–67.

20. For a list of the molecules, see Iain Gilmour and Mark A. Sephton, eds., *An Introduction to Astrobiology* (New York: The Open University, Cambridge University Press, 2004): 16.

21. L. E. Snyder et al., "A Rigorous Attempt to Verify Interstellar Glycine," *Astrophysical Journal* 619 (February 1, 2005): 914–30; Yi-Jehng Kuan et al., "A Search for Interstellar Pyrimidine," *Monthly Notices of the Royal Astronomical Society* 345 (October 2003): 650–56.

22. Keith A. Kvenvolden, "Chirality of Amino Acids in the Murchison Meteorite—A Historical Perspective," in *ISSOL '99: 12th International Conference on the Origin of Life: Book of Program and Abstracts*, comp. and ed. Lois Lane (La Jolla, CA: University of California, San Diego, 1999), 41; Daniel P. Glavin et al., "Amino Acids in Martian Meteorite Nakhla," in *ISSOL '99*, 62; Sandra Pizzarello et al., "The Organic Content of the Taglish Lake Meteorite," *Science* 293 (September 21, 2001): 2239nn15, 28.

23. For a review of the homochirality problem, see Rana and Ross, *Origins of Life*, 123–33.

24. Francis Crick and Leslie E. Orgel, "Directed Panspermia," *Icarus* 19 (July 1973): 341–46. Francis Crick later wrote a full-length book on the hypothesis, *Life Itself: Its Nature and Origin* (New York: Simon & Schuster, 1981).

25. Stenger, *God: The Failed Hypothesis*, 155.

26. Ibid., 161.

27. Ibid.

28. Ibid., 160.

29. Kenneth Richard Samples, "The Historic Christian View of Man," in *A World of Difference: Putting Christian Truth-Claims to the Worldview Test* (Grand Rapids: Baker, 2007), 171–88.

30. Carl Sagan, *Cosmos* (New York: Random House, 1980), 4. This quote is the opening sentence in Carl Sagan's book and the opening comment in his thirteen-episode *Cosmos* series that was first broadcast in 1980 on the Public Broadcasting Service television network. Cosmos Studios in Los Angeles released a remastered and visually updated DVD set in 2002.

31. In Genesis 1:28–30 God commanded the first humans he had created, Adam and Eve, to multiply and fill the Earth so that their descendents could wisely manage the resources of the entire planet for the benefit of all life.

32. See Genesis 18:1–16, 19:1–22; Numbers 20:16; Daniel 3:16–29, 6:16–23, 7:15–28, 8:15–27, 9:20–27, 10:4–21; Zechariah 1:9–6:8; Matthew 1:20–24, 2:13, 19–20; Luke 1:11–20, 1:26–38, 2:8–15; Acts 5:19–21, 8:26, 10:1–8, 12:6–11, 27:23–26; Revelation 5:1–5, 7:1–12, 8:1, 10:11, 14:6–19, 17:1–18:24, 19:9–10, 21:9–21, 22:1–6.

Chapter 5: Why Such a Dark Universe?

1. Astronomer Guillermo Gonzalez and science historian Jay W. Richards wrote an entire book on the supernatural design of the universe and solar system for facilitating human observation of the structure and history of the universe: *The Privileged Planet: How Our Place in the Cosmos Is Designed for Discovery.*

In this chapter I have sought to augment the evidence on which their conclusion is based.

2. Keiko Atobe, Shigeru Ida, and Takashi Ito, "Obliquity Variations of Terrestrial Planets in Habitable Zones," *Icarus* 168 (April 2004): 223–36; William R. Ward, "Comments on the Long-Term Stability of the Earth's Obliquity," *Icarus* 50 (May–June 1982): 444–48; Carl D. Murray, "Seasoned Travelers," *Nature* 361 (February 18, 1993): 586–87; Jacques Laskar, F. Joutel, and P. Robutel, "Stabilization of the Earth's Obliquity by the Moon," *Nature* 361 (February 18, 1993): 615–17.

3. Atobe, Ida, and Ito, "Obliquity Variations," 223–36; Jacques Laskar and P. Robutel, "The Chaotic Obliquity of the Planets," *Nature* 361 (February 18, 1993): 608–12.

4. Dave Waltham, "Anthropic Selection for the Moon's Mass," *Astrobiology* 4 (December 2004): 460–68.

5. Ibid.

6. Neil F. Comins, *What If the Moon Didn't Exist? Voyages to Earths That Might Have Been* (New York: HarperCollins, 1993).

7. Henry Norris Russell, "On the Albedo of the Planets and Their Satellites," *Proceedings of the National Academy of Sciences, USA* 2 (February 15, 1916): 74–77. Also available at http://www.pnas.org/content/vol2/issue2/ (accessed January 21, 2008).

8. E. Komatsu et al., "Five-Year Wilkinson Microwave Anisotropy Probe (WMAP) Observations: Cosmological Interpretation," (preprint, National Aeronautics and Space Administration, 2008): http://lambda.gsfc.nasa.gov/product/map/dr3/pub_papers/fiveyear/cosmology/wmap_5yr_cosmo.pdf.

9. Ibid.

Chapter 6: Why a Decaying Universe?

1. The rate of decay, or entropy, is a measure of the degree to which energy in a closed system dissipates as heat, and thus ceases to be available to perform work. Specific entropy is the amount of entropy per proton. A familiar high-entropy system would be a candle flame. Its specific entropy = 2. A supernova explosion's specific entropy = 10,000,000. The universe as a whole is the most entropic system known. Its specific entropy exceeds 100,000,000.

2. Sir William Thomson (Lord Kelvin), "On the Dynamical Theory of Heat, with Numerical Results Deduced from Mr. Joule's Equivalent of a Thermal Unit, and M. Regnault's Observations on Steam," (1851) in *Mathematical and Physical Papers* 1 (Cambridge: Cambridge University Press, 1882), 175–83, http://zapatopi.net/kelvin/papers/on_the_dynamical_theory_of_heat.html (accessed August 13, 2007); Sir William Thomson (Lord Kelvin), "On a Universal Tendency in Nature to the Dissipation of Mechanical Energy" (1852), in *Mathematical and Physical Papers* 1, 511–18, http://zapatopi.net/kelvin/papers/on_a_universal_tendency.html (accessed August 13, 2007).

3. Sir Arthur Eddington, *The Nature of the Physical World* (Cambridge: Cambridge University Press, 1928); Sir James Jeans, "The Physics of the Universe," *Nature* 122 (November 3, 1928): 689–700.

4. Robert A. Millikan, "Available Energy," *Science* 68 (September 28, 1928): 283.

5. An example would be the book by astrophysicist Paul Davies titled *The Last Three Minutes: Conjectures about the Ultimate Fate of the Universe* (New York: Basic, 1994).

6. Lawrence M. Krauss and Glenn D. Starkman, "Life, the Universe, and Nothing: Life and Death in an Ever-Expanding Universe," *Astrophysical Journal* 531 (March 1, 2000): 22–30.

7. Sagan, *Cosmos*, 4.

8. Adam G. Riess et al., "Observational Evidence from Supernovae for an Accelerating Universe and a Cosmological Constant," *Astronomical Journal* 116 (September 1998): 1009–38; S. Perlmutter et al., "Measurements of Ω and from 42 High-Redshift Supernovae," *Astrophysical Journal* 517 (June 1, 1999): 565–86.

9. D. N. Spergel et al., "Three-Year *Wilkinson Microwave Anisotropy Probe* (*WMAP*) Observations: Implications for Cosmology," 377–408. E. Komatsu et al., "Five-Year Wilkinson Microwave Anisotropy Probe (WMAP) Observations."

10. "The Affirmations of Humanism: A Statement of Principles," *Free Inquiry*, Fall 2002, 2. The statements appear on the inside cover of each issue of *Free Inquiry*.

11. Sagan, *Cosmos*, 4.

Chapter 7: Why a Realm beyond This One?

1. Curtis S. Cooper and Alexander A. Pavlov, "P-16. A New Twist on Planetary Habitability," *Astrobiology* 7 (June 2007): 507.

2. Q. R. Ahmad et al., "Measurement of the Rate of $v_e + d \rightarrow p + p + e^-$ Interactions Produced by ^{8}B Solar Neutrinos at the Sudbury Neutrino Observatory," *Physical Review Letters* 87 (August 13, 2001): 71301(6); A. B. Balantekin and H. Yüksel, "Do the KamLAND and Solar Neutrino Data Rule Out Solar Density Fluctuations?" *Physical Review* D 68 (July 1, 2003): 013006.

3. F. W. Dyson, A. S. Eddington, and C. Davidson, "A Determination of the Deflection of Light by the Sun's Gravitational Field, from Observations Made at the Total Eclipse of May 29, 1919," *Philosophical Transactions of the Royal Society of London* A 220 (June 1920): 291–333.

4. Ward and Brownlee, *Rare Earth*, 194–234.

5. Fazale Rana with Hugh Ross, *Who Was Adam? A Creation Model Approach to the Origin of Man* (Colorado Springs: NavPress, 2005), 97–109.

6. Brandon Carter, "The Anthropic Principle and Its Implications for Biological Evolution," *Philosophical Transactions of the Royal Society of London* A 310 (December 20, 1983): 347–63.

7. John D. Barrow and Frank J. Tipler, *The Anthropic Cosmological Principle* (New York: Oxford University Press, 1986), 556–70.

8. Ibid.

9. Adam Eyre-Walker and Peter D. Keightley, "High Genomic Deleterious Mutation Rates in Hominids," *Nature* 397 (January 28, 1999): 344–47; James F. Crow, "The Odds of Losing at Genetic Roulette," *Nature* 397 (January 28, 1999):

293–94; Hugh Ross, "Aliens from Another World? Getting Here from There," *Facts for Faith*, no. 6, second quarter 2001, 30–31.

10. Fazale R. Rana, *The Cell's Design: How Chemistry Reveals the Creator's Artistry* (Grand Rapids: Baker, 2008); Rana and Ross, *Origins of Life*.

11. Religious relics and undisputed burial rituals date back at least 22,000–30,000 years. See Richard G. Klein, *The Human Career: Human Biological and Cultural Origins*, 2nd ed. (Chicago: University of Chicago Press, 1999), 550–53; Rana and Ross, *Who Was Adam?* 90–91.

12. "Major Religions of the World Ranked by Number of Adherents," Adherents.com, August 9, 2007, http:www.adherents.com/Religions_By_Adherents.html; "Worldwide Adherents of All Religions by Six Continental Areas, Mid-1995," zpub.com, http:www.zpub.com/un/pope/relig.html (accessed December 22, 2007); B. A. Robinson, "Religions of the World," ReligiousTolerance.org, July 19, 2007, http:www.religioustolerance.org/worldrel.htm. These databases note that only 2.5–3.8 percent of the world's population identifies itself as atheistic. An additional 5–8 percent is identified as agnostic.

Chapter 8: Why This Particular Planet, Star, Galaxy, and Universe?

1. Ross, *Creator and the Cosmos*, 157–74.

Chapter 9: Why Believe the Bible?

1. For a more extensive description of the Bible's cosmological content, see the author's book *A Matter of Days: Resolving a Creation Controversy* (Colorado Springs: NavPress, 2004), 139–48.

2. These books include Ross, *The Creator and the Cosmos: How the Greatest Scientific Discoveries of the Century Reveal God*, 3rd ed.; Rana and Ross, *Origins of Life: Biblical and Evolutionary Models Face Off*; Rana with Ross, *Who Was Adam? A Creation Model Approach to the Origin of Man*; Ross, *Creation as Science: A Testable Model Approach to End the Creation/Evolution Wars*; Hugh Ross, *The Genesis Question: Scientific Advances and the Accuracy of Genesis*, 2nd ed. (Colorado Springs: NavPress, 2001); Ross, *Beyond the Cosmos: The Extra-Dimensionality of God; What Recent Discoveries in Astrophysics Reveal about the Glory and Love of God*.

3. This impossibility refers to created life. The creator of time, the triune God (Father, Son, and Holy Spirit), is in no way limited by time.

4. R. Laird Harris, Gleason L. Archer, and Bruce K. Waltke, *Theological Wordbook of the Old Testament* 1 (Chicago: Moody, 1980), 127.

5. Some latter-day holy books like the Qur'an (e.g., 7:54, 10:3, 11:7, 25:59, 32:4, 50:38, 57:4) and the Mormon text *Pearl of Great Price* (e.g., Moses 2–4 and Abraham 4–5) copy the concept from the Bible but also include teachings that are inconsistent with that information (e.g., 41:9–12 in the Qur'an and Moses 1 and Abraham 3 in *Pearl of Great Price*).

6. This achievement is described in considerable detail in two of my books: *The Fingerprint of God*, 39–118; *Creator and the Cosmos*, 31–136.

7. Stephen Hawking and Roger Penrose, "The Singularities of Gravitational Collapse and Cosmology," *Proceedings of the Royal Society of London* A 314 (January 27, 1970): 529–48.

8. Roger Penrose, *Shadows of the Mind: A Search for the Missing Science of Consciousness* (New York: Oxford University Press, 1994), 230.

9. Arvind Borde and Alexander Vilenkin, "Eternal Inflation and the Initial Singularity," *Physical Review Letters* 72 (May 23, 1994): 3305–8; Arvind Borde, "Open and Closed Universes, Initial Singularities, and Inflation," *Physical Review* D 50 (September 15, 1994): 3692–3702; Arvind Borde and Alexander Vilenkin, "Singularities in Inflationary Cosmology: A Review," *International Journal of Modern Physics* D 5 (December 1996): 813–24; Arvind Borde and Alexander Vilenkin, "Violation of the Weak Energy Condition in Inflating Spacetimes," *Physical Review* D 56 (July 15, 1997): 717–23; Arvind Borde, Alan H. Guth, and Alexander Vilenkin, "Inflationary Spacetimes Are Incomplete in Past Directions," *Physical Review Letters* 90 (April 18, 2003): id. 151301.

10. At the suggestion of and with the assistance of John Rea, professor emeritus of Old Testament at Regent University, I wrote an article describing the biblical context for big bang cosmology. Three versions of the article, "Big Bang—The Bible Taught It First," exist. They can be found in *Creator and the Cosmos*, 23–29; in *A Matter of Days*, 139–48; and on the RTB website at http://www.reasons.org/resources/fff/2000issue03/index.shtml#big_bang_the_bible_taught_it_first.

11. For a philosophical response to this question, see Kenneth Richard Samples, "If God Created All Things, Who Created God?" *Connections*, fourth quarter 2007, 6–7. This article is also available at http://www.reasons.org/resources/connections (accessed December 18, 2007).

12. Richard Dawkins and Jerry Coyne, "One Side Can Be Wrong," *The Guardian Unlimited*, September 1, 2005, http://www.guardian.co.uk/science/2005/sep/01/schools.research.

13. Some recently composed holy books such as the Qur'an and the Mormon scriptures incorporate verbatim hundreds of Bible verses into their texts.

14. See Ross, *Beyond the Cosmos*, 53–62, 73–79, 117–30.

15. The phrase "like a tent" in Psalm 104:2 and in Isaiah 40:22 is a simile. These passages imply that God's stretching out of the heavens resembles in some ways, but is not precisely equivalent to, the unfolding of a tent.

16. Antoinette Songaila et al., "Measurement of the Microwave Background Temperature at Redshift 1.776," *Nature* 371 (1994): 43–45; David M. Meyer, "A Distant Space Thermometer," *Nature* 371 (1994): 13; K. C. Roth et al., "C I Fine-Structure Excitation by the CMBR at $z = 1.973$," *American Astronomical Society Meeting 189, #122.17, Bulletin of the American Astronomical Society* 29 (January 1997): 736; R. Srianand, P. Petitjean, and C. Leadoux, "The Cosmic Microwave Background Radiation Temperature at Redshift 2.74," *Nature* 408 (2000): 931–35; P. Molaro, S. S. Levshakov, M. Dessauges-Zavadsky, and S. D'Odorico, "The Cosmic Microwave Radiation Temperature at $z = 3.025$ Toward QSO 0347–3819," *Astronomy and Astrophysics* 381 (2002): L64–L67; E. S. Battistelli et al., "Cosmic Microwave Background Temperature at Galaxy Clusters," *Astrophysical Journal Letters* 580 (2002): L101–L104; D. J. Fixsen and J. C. Mather, "The Spectral Results of the Far-Infrared Absolute Spectrophotometer Instrument on COBE,"

Astrophysical Journal 581 (2002): 817–22; J. C. Mather et al., "Calibrator Design for the COBE Far-Infrared Absolute Spectrophotometer (FIRAS)," *Astrophysical Journal* 512 (1999): 511–20; J. C. Mather et al., "Measurement of the Cosmic Microwave Background Spectrum by the COBE FIRAS Instrument," *Astrophysical Journal* 420 (1994): 439–44; Katherine C. Roth, David M. Meyer, and Isabel Hawkins, "Interstellar Cyanogen and the Temperature of the Cosmic Microwave Background Radiation," *Astrophysical Journal* 413 (1993): L67–L71.

17. One of the greatest engineering feats of all time is a gravity wave telescope that was designed by Caltech and MIT physicists and financed by United States taxpayers. This instrument has the capability of making length measurements with an accuracy of one part in 10^{23}. One part in 10^{23}, however, ranks at least 10^{97} times (ten million quadrillion quadrillion quadrillion quadrillion quadrillion quadrillion times) inferior to the level of fine-tuning in the dark energy parameter that is necessary to make physical life possible in the universe. This fine-tuning difference, based on only one cosmic design parameter, implies that the cosmic causal Agent at a minimum is 10^{97} times more intelligent, more knowledgeable, and more creative than Caltech and MIT physicists. It also implies that the cosmic causal Agent is at least 10^{97} times better funded or more powerful than the United States federal government. The differences between the Agent's and humanity's capabilities become even more dramatic when one includes the dozens of other cosmic characteristics manifesting exquisite fine-tuning. See LIGO: Laser Interferometer Gravitational-Wave Observatory, http://www.ligo.caltech.edu/ (accessed January 25, 2008).

18. John N. Bahcall, Charles L. Steinhardt, and David Schlegel, "Does the Fine-Structure Constant Vary with Cosmological Epoch?" *Astrophysical Journal* 600 (January 10, 2004): 520–43; P. C. W. Davies, Tamara M. Davis, and Charles H. Lineweaver, "Black Holes Constrain Varying Constants," *Nature* 418 (August 8, 2002): 602–3; Alexander Y. Potekhin et al., "Testing Cosmological Variability of the Proton-to-Electron Mass Ratio Using the Spectrum of PKS 0528–250," *Astrophysical Journal* 505 (October 1, 1998): 523–28; D. B. Guenther, L. M. Krauss, and P. Demarque, "Testing the Constancy of the Gravitational Constant Using Helioseismology," *Astrophysical Journal* 498 (May 10, 1998): 871–76; E. Peik et al., "Limit on the Present Temporal Variation of the Fine Structure Constant," *Physical Review Letters* 93 (October 18, 2004), doi:10.1103/PhysRevLett.93.170801, http://link.aps.org/abstract/PRL/v93/e170801.

19. Robin M. Canup, "Simulations of a Late Lunar-Forming Impact," *Icarus* 168 (April 2004): 433–56; Herbert Palme, "The Giant Impact Formation of the Moon," *Science* 304 (May 14, 2004): 977–79; Stein B. Jacobsen, "The Hf-W Isotopic System and the Origin of the Earth and Moon," *Annual Review of Earth and Planetary Sciences* 33 (May 2005): 531–70; Keiichi Wada, Eiichiro Kokubo, and Junichiro Makino, "High-Resolution Simulations of a Moon-Forming Impact and Postimpact Evolution," *Astrophysical Journal* 638 (February 20, 2006): 1180–86.

20. Kevin A. Maher and David J. Stevenson, "Impact Frustration of the Origin of Life," *Nature* 331 (February 18, 1988): 612–14; Verne R. Oberbeck and Guy Fogleman, "Impacts and the Origin of Life," *Nature* 339 (June 8, 1989): 434; Norman H. Sleep et al., "Annihilation of Ecosystems by Large Asteroid Impacts on the Early Earth," *Nature* 342 (November 9, 1989): 139–42.

21. Rana and Ross, *Origins of Life*, 81–105.

22. Ibid., 40–44.

23. The Hebrew word used here, *nepesh*, is not to be confused with the New Testament concept of soul, based on the Greek word *psuchē*. A person's *psuchē* (soul) and *pneuma* (spirit) are inseparably united, in the Greek conception. The Old Testament references to birds and mammals as "soulish" creatures in no way imply that these creatures possess spiritual attributes.

24. Ross, *The Genesis Question*, 49–54.

25. Paul and Anne Ehrlich made this claim in 1981 in their book *Extinction: The Causes and Consequences of the Disappearance of a Species* (New York: Ballantine, 1981), 33. Since then biologists have challenged their claim but have been able to do so only by appealing to examples of plant speciation, forced breeding experiments (in the laboratory) on insects, pupa emergence time differentiation in some insect species caused by human introduction of a secondary food source, or field observations of birds and rodents where the subpopulations from a single species choose not to breed with one another (for anti-creation sources see Joseph Boxhorn, "Observed Instances of Speciation," The TalkOrigins Archive, September 1, 1995, http://www.talkorigins.org/faqs/faq-speciation.html, and Chris Stassen et al., "Some More Observed Speciation Events," The TalkOrigins Archive, http://www.talkorigins.org/faqs/speciation.html [accessed December 16, 2007]). These challenges are out of context in that they rest on narrow definitions of a species rather than on the broad definition used by the Ehrlichs (over a dozen different definitions for "species" exist in the scientific literature) or appeal to human interference or to non-animal examples. To put it another way, while scientists can cite numerous examples of natural macro-extinction events (for animals) observed in real time, they cannot produce examples for similarly qualified macro-speciation events.

26. For description and documentation of this evidence, see Rana and Ross, *Who Was Adam?* 77–95.

27. Rana and Ross, *Who Was Adam?*

28. Guido de Brès, "The Belgic Confession," in *Ecumenical Creeds and Reformed Confessions* (Grand Rapids: CRC Publications, 1988), 79.

29. Galileo identifies Cardinal Baronius as the author of the quote in note 8 of "Galileo Galilei, Letter to Madame Christina of Lorraine, Grand Duchess of Tuscany: Concerning the Use of Biblical Quotations in Matters of Science (1615)," Stillman Drake, trans., *Interdisciplinary Documentation on Religion and Science*, http://www.disf.org/en/documentation/03–Galileo_Cristina.asp (accessed January 19, 2008).

Chapter 10: Why Not a Perfect Universe—Now?

1. B. J. Carr, "On the Origin, Evolution and Purpose of the Physical Universe," in *Physical Cosmology and Philosophy*, ed. John Leslie (New York: Macmillan, 1990), 148–52; Richard Swinburne, "Argument from the Fine-Tuning of the Universe," in *Physical Cosmology and Philosophy*, 154–64; George V. Coyne, "Some Theological Reflections on the Anthropic Principle," in *The Anthropic Principle: Proceedings of the Second Venice Conference on Cosmology and Philosophy*, ed.

F. Bertola and U. Curi (Cambridge: Cambridge University Press, 1993), 162–67; Edward Harrison, *Masks of the Universe* (New York: Collier Books, Macmillan, 1985), 249–52.

2. Ross, *The Creator and the Cosmos*, 145–99; Hugh Ross, Kenneth Samples, and Mark Clark, *Lights in the Sky and Little Green Men*, 171–92. For links to resources on design evidence, see "Frequently Asked Questions: Evidence for Design," Reasons To Believe, http://www.reasons.org/resources/apologetics/index.shtml#design_in_the_universe (accessed May 23, 2006).

3. See Revelation 21:3–5, 21:10–22:5, and Ross, *Beyond the Cosmos*, 219–22.

4. See Revelation 21:22–22:5, and Ross, *Beyond the Cosmos*, 222–23.

5. See Revelation 21:3–22:5, and Ross, *Beyond the Cosmos*, 223–28.

6. This Christian doctrine finds considerable support from secular research scientists. An example would be two books by Roger Penrose: *The Emperor's New Mind: Concerning Computers, Minds, and the Laws of Physics* (New York: Oxford University Press, 1989), and *Shadows of the Mind*.

7. Some theologians dispute the reference of this passage to Lucifer.

8. While I cannot emphasize enough the importance of reading and studying the entire Bible, I sometimes urge people newly exploring life's big questions to read in one sitting the first three chapters of Genesis, all of Romans, and the last three chapters of Revelation.

9. Rana, *The Cell's Design*.

10. See "The Shorter Catechism with the Scripture Proofs," Creeds of Christendom, February 1996, http://www.creeds.net/reformed/Westminster/shorter_catechism.html. The following Bible passages are listed in support of the answer: Psalm 16:5–11; 86:9; 144:15; Isaiah 12:2; 60:21; Luke 2:10; Romans 11:36; 1 Corinthians 6:20; 10:31; Philippians 4:4; Revelation 4:11; 21:3–4.

11. Of the 15,000 to 20,000 bird species present on Earth at the time of humanity's origin, only about 9,000 still remain. Of approximately 8,000 land mammal species, only about 4,000 still remain. See Gary K. Meffe, C. Ronald Carroll, and contributors, *Principles of Conservation Biology*, 2nd ed. (Sunderland, MA: Sinauer Associates, 1997), 87–156; John Alroy, "A Multispecies Overkill Simulation of the End-Pleistocene Megafaunal Mass Extinction," *Science* 292 (June 8, 2001): 1893–96; Richard G. Roberts et al., "New Ages for the Last Australian Megafauna: Continent-Wide Extinction About 46,000 Years Ago," *Science* 292 (June 8, 2001): 1888–92; Paul R. Ehrlich and Anne H. Ehrlich, *Extinction: The Causes and Consequences of the Disappearance of a Species*, 20–21; Jeffrey K. McKee et al., "Forecasting Global Biodiversity Threats Associated with Human Population Growth," *Biological Conservation* 115 (January 2004): 161–64; Leigh Dayton, "Mass Extinctions Pinned on Ice Age Hunters," *Science* 292 (June 8, 2001): 1819; Gerardo Ceballos and Paul R. Ehrlich, "Mammal Population Losses and the Extinction Crisis," *Science* 296 (May 3, 2002): 904–7; David W. Steadman, "Prehistoric Extinctions of Pacific Island Birds: Biodiversity Meets Zooarchaeology," *Science* 267 (February 24, 1995): 1123–31; "Human Impact on the Earth: Journey into New Worlds," *The Sacred Balance: A Vision of Humanity's Place in Nature*, http://www.sacredbalance.com/web/drilldown.html?sku=35 (accessed June 29, 2005); "The Late Pleistocene Extinctions," The Savory Center, http://www.holisticmanagement.org/oll_late.cfm?cfid=834659&cftoken=58449918 (accessed

June 29, 2005, site now discontinued). In North and South America and Australia the large mammal extinction rate during the human occupation period stands at 73, 79, and 86 percent, respectively. See Christopher Stringer and Robin McKie, *African Exodus: The Origins of Humanity* (New York: Henry Holt, 1997), 165–66; Paul S. Martin and Richard G. Klein, eds., *Quaternary Extinctions: A Prehistoric Revolution* (Tucson: University of Arizona Press, 1984).

12. In Genesis 1:28–30 Adam and Eve and their descendants were commanded to "subdue" by managing all of Earth's resources not only for their advantage but also for the benefit of all Earth's life.

13. Ann Gibbons, "Calibrating the Mitochondrial Clock," *Science* 279 (January 2, 1998): 28–29; Lois A. Tully et al., "A Sensitive Denaturing Gradient-Gel Electrophoresis Assay Reveals a High Frequency of Heteroplasmy in Hypervariable Region 1 of the Human mtDNA Control Region," *American Journal of Human Genetics* 67 (August 2000): 432–43; Hugh Ross and Sam Conner, "Eve's Secret to Growing Younger," *Facts & Faith*, first quarter 1998, 1–2; Jonathan K. Pritchard et al., "Population Growth of Human Y Chromosomes: A Study of Y Chromosome Microsatellites," *Molecular Biology and Evolution* 16 (December 1999): 1791–98; Russell Thomson et al., "Recent Common Ancestry of Human Y Chromosomes: Evidence from DNA Sequence Data," *Proceedings of the National Academy of Sciences, USA* 97 (June 2000): 7360–65; Peter A. Underhill et al., "Y Chromosome Sequence Variation and the History of Human Populations," *Nature Genetics* 26 (November 2000): 358–61; L. Simon Whitfield, John E. Sulston, and Peter N. Goodfellow, "Sequence Variation of the Human Y Chromosome," *Nature* 378 (November 23, 1995): 379–80. For the anthropological evidence see the citations in Fazale Rana with Hugh Ross, *Who Was Adam?* 55–95.

14. Barrow and Tipler, *The Anthropic Cosmological Principle*, 556–70. The promise made in the New Testament is that Jesus Christ the Creator will return to Earth to wrap up the conquest and removal of evil as soon as his followers complete their assignment, called "The Great Commission" (see Matthew 28:18–20; Acts 1:6–8; and Revelation 19–21). The term refers to Jesus's final command to make disciples among all people groups in the world. Ralph Winter, executive director of the U.S. Center for World Mission, in his lectures and writings, says Christians already possess the necessary technology, financial resources, and personnel to finish the job. All that's lacking is sufficient motivation and willingness to sacrifice. See "The Amazing Countdown Facts," United States Center for World Missions, http://www.uscwm.org/mobilization_division/resources/web_articles_11–20–01/ Amazing%20Countdown%20Facts.pdf (accessed January 18, 2008).

Chapter 11: Why These Physical Laws and Dimensions?

1. D. M. Murphy et al., "Influence of Sea-Salt on Aerosol Radiative Properties in the Southern Ocean Marine Boundary Layer," *Nature* 392 (March 5, 1998): 62–65.

2. Ruprecht Jaenicke, "Abundance of Cellular Material and Proteins in the Atmosphere," *Science* 308 (April 1, 2005): 73.

3. Nicholas R. Bates, Anthony H. Knap, and Anthony F. Michaels, "Contribution of Hurricanes to Local and Global Estimates of Air-Sea Exchange of CO_2," *Nature* 395 (September 3, 1998): 58–61.

4. For documentation see my earlier book *Creation as Science*, 165–74.

5. The Old Testament documents occasions when God used natural disasters as tools of judgment or as calls to repentance, but that occurred only when the expression of evil became egregious and concentrated. For example, see the account of Deborah and Barak in Judges 4–5.

6. "Art of the First Cities: Writing: Mesopotamia," The Metropolitan Museum of Art, http://www.metmuseum.org/explore/First_Cities/writing_meso_object_330R.htm (accessed April 16, 2005). These genealogies record life spans in rounded-off numbers, and in some cases the life spans are listed as ten times longer than those documented in Genesis 5 and 11.

7. For an explanation as to how these life spans could be so long, see Ross, *The Genesis Question*, 117–25, and Rana and Ross, *Who Was Adam?* 111–21.

8. See Ross, *The Genesis Question*, 127–87.

9. See "Wildland Fire in Yellowstone," National Park Service, http://www.nps.gov/yell/naturescience/wildlandfire.htm (accessed January 28, 2008).

10. The moral standard dictated by God and by our conscience is summarized in Matthew 5:17–7:23.

11. The Westminster Shorter Catechism of 1674 lists as its first question and first answer the following: "What is the chief end of man?" "Man's chief end is to glorify God, and to enjoy him forever." "The Shorter Catechism with the Scripture Proofs," Creeds of Christendom, February 1996, http://www.creeds.net/reformed/Westminster/shorter_catechism.html.

12. Sagan, *Cosmos*, 4.

Chapter 12: Why Two Creations?

1. The Bible does not specify when in relation to the universe God created the angels. According to Job 38:4–7, the angels were present, however, at the laying of Earth's foundations.

2. For the scientific and biblical details of all that God did to prepare life and the Earth for humanity, see my book *Creation as Science*.

3. See also Ross, *Beyond the Cosmos*, 151–93.

4. Ibid.

Chapter 13: Why Is the New Creation Better?

1. Hebrews 12:18–29 contrasts the earthly Jerusalem with the heavenly Jerusalem.

2. Note also that Revelation 21 and 22 refer to the assembly of human believers with both singular and plural nouns.

3. Joseph Henry Thayer, trans., *A Greek-English Lexicon of the New Testament*, rev. ed. (Grand Rapids: Baker, 1977), 360–61.

4. The duration of the seventh day of the Genesis creation week, the day on which God rested from creating, is a matter of heated debate among Christians.

Some say the seventh day lasted twenty-four hours. Others interpret it as a long but finite period. Others see it as continuing through all eternity. The concept of an eighth creation day as the beginning of the new creation described in Revelation 21 and 22 is unique to the day-age perspective and certain other old-earth creationist positions. For a written exchange on the topic, see David Hagopian, ed., *The Genesis Debate: Three Views on the Days of Creation* (Mission Viejo, CA: Crux), 2001.

5. Nathan J. Emery and Nicola S. Clayton, "The Mentality of Crows: Convergent Evolution of Intelligence in Corvids and Apes," *Science* 306 (December 10, 2004): 1903–7.

Appendix B: Where Is the Cosmic Density Fine-Tuning?

1. Spergel et al., "Three-Year *Wilkinson Microwave Anisotropy Probe (WMAP)* Observations," 397–98. E. Komatsu et al., "Five-Year Wilkinson Microwave Anisotropy Probe (WMAP) Observations."

2. Spergel et al., "Three Year *Wilkinson Microwave Anisotropy Probe (WMAP)* Observations," 392–94.

Index

Index

Index